MUSICAL CHILDHOODS

Musical Childhoods is a culmination of more than a decade of research driven by the fact that music has been neglected in early childhood programmes in favour of literacy and numeracy. Recent research has identified a connection between academic performance and musical programmes and this has given music a renewed status in many schools.

This book promotes the idea of children's competence in the use of the language of music and argues that all children have a right to participate in musical discovery, celebrating children's engagement with meaningful and disparate experiences in music. Written by leading practitioners and researchers in the field, this book seeks to reaffirm children's communicative competence when exposed to high-quality musical experience, provide new perspectives on children's ability to engage with music in many diverse forms and explore and promote the role of the musician as an artist and teacher.

The book is structured in three parts:

- The theoretical overview
- The children, the musicians and the music
- The research through the eyes of the protagonist and looking into the future.

Early childhood students, researchers and academics with a specific interest in music and musicality will find this an insightful read.

Berenice Nyland is Associate Professor in early childhood at RMIT University in the School of Education, Australia.

Aleksandra Acher is a ter in music and early childhood academic in the School of Educa on

Jill Ferris is a practising musician. She has been a music educator and a lecturer in music education at the School of Education, RMIT University, Australia.

Jan Deans is Senior Lecturer in early childhood and Director of the Early Learning Centre at the University of Melbourne, Australia.

MUSICAL CHILDHOODS

Explorations in the pre-school years

Berenice Nyland, Aleksandra Acker, Jill Ferris and Jan Deans

Routledge
Taylor & Francis Group

LONDON AND NEW YORK

First published 2015
by Routledge
2 Park Square, Milton Park, Abingdon, Oxon OX14 4RN

and by Routledge
711 Third Avenue, New York, NY 10017

Routledge is an imprint of the Taylor & Francis Group, an informa business

British Library Cataloguing in Publication Data
A catalogue record for this book is available from the British Library

Library of Congress Cataloging-in-Publication Data
Musical childhoods : explorations in the pre-school years / Berenice Nyland,
Jill Ferris, Aleksandra Acker and Jan Deans.
pages cm
ISBN 978-0-415-74005-0 (hardback) – ISBN 978-0-415-74006-7 (pbk.) –
ISBN 978-1-315-81467-4 (e-book) 1. Music–Instruction and study–Juvenile.
2. Education, Preschool. I. Nyland, Berenice. II. Acker, Aleksandra.
III. Ferris, Jill. IV. Deans, Jan.
MT1.M987363 2014
372.87–dc23
2014034735

ISBN: 978-0-415-74005-0 (hbk)
ISBN: 978-0-415-74006-7 (pbk)
ISBN: 978-1-315-81467-4 (ebk)

Typeset in Bembo
by Cenveo Publisher Services

Printed and bound in Great Britain by
TJ International Ltd, Padstow, Cornwall

DEDICATION

We would like to dedicate this book to the children, families and staff of the Early Learning Centre. All participated generously in the research described here. The musicians allowed themselves to be observed and shared their plans and reflections, while participating staff were always welcoming and supported the research in many ways. For example, their own digital recordings of music sessions were shared and when asked about attending interviews all were willing to give up the time. The interview transcripts are also indicative of thoughtful contemplation about the programme and the differing roles. The children are especially remembered for their unique responses to the events described here and their good-hearted collaboration with adults and each other. Their freshness of approach and ability to be playful made this research a pleasure. The parents' enthusiasm for the music was also an essential part of this ongoing initiative.

CONTENTS

FIGURES

TABLES

ACKNOWLEDGEMENTS

We would like to acknowledge Jan Deans, an author of this book, the director at the Early Learning Centre and a major protagonist in the music programme. As well as the designing the arts programme at the centre, Jan organised and managed many of the initiatives observed. She organised access for the external researchers, was part of the research team and liaised between centre staff and researchers so we were always welcome and received wonderful support. Lesley Dunn, Leah Raymond and Kylie Payman, the three musicians, were generous with their expertise and time, and trusted the researchers to observe their practice. We would like to thank them for letting us into their sessions and sharing so openly. For specialists to be observed constantly must be a strain at times, but we were never made to feel we were anything but welcome. The music, the responses of the children and the thought and effort that went into these sessions were an amazing experience for us. To Suzana Klarin we owe a special debt in that she was able to celebrate the music in and around the centre in an enthusiastic way that created new opportunities. Her skilled provocations to the children resulted in unexpected outcomes and her curriculum document, where she recorded her pedagogical explorations, was splendid. Also to our colleagues, especially David Forrest, who have been a constant support.

ABBREVIATION AND TERMINOLOGY

The site of the research was an early learning centre, which has been referred to as the ELC and the centre throughout the document.

The term 'home-room' refers to what can alternatively be described as a 'nursery class'.

PART I

The context

1

YOUNG CHILDREN, MUSIC AND EARLY CHILDHOOD PROGRAMMES

Introduction

The book *Musical Childhoods: Explorations in the Pre-school Years* is a culmination of more than a decade of research carried out in an early learning centre in Australia. The research was driven by two circumstances. The first one was that music in Australian early childhood programmes had been neglected as literacy and numeracy attained a privileged position. A report called *Augmenting the Diminished* (DEST, 2005) highlighted this situation in primary schools and smaller studies have suggested the same circumstances exist in early childhood educational settings (Anderson, 2002). The influence of the Reggio Emilia philosophy on early childhood programmes in Australia was the second driver in this research. From Reggio Emilia has come the idea of the '100 languages of children' and a renewed interest in the arts was sparked in tertiary courses and in many early childhood settings.

The neglected position of early childhood music in tertiary education courses has been researched (Ferris and Nyland, 2007) and it was found that many universities no longer had stand-alone subjects for music and some had no arts offerings at all. A number of Australian music researchers had reported on the impact this had on daily practice within early childhood centres. De Vries (2006, 2013) carried out studies on early childhood teachers' use of recorded music, Suthers (2004) reported on the lack of confidence teachers displayed in the area of providing for music and Barrett wondered why visual art seemed easier to provide for than music (1993). For many children, their daily musical experiences consist of recorded music, often used for ritual activities, such as clean up time, or basic dance sessions consisting of such pursuits as free movement to early childhood music – for example, *The Wiggles*. Suthers' research reported that many teachers had no trust in their ability to 'sing in tune' and for many services even the daily sing-a-long has ceased to happen.

The second impetus to explore the presence of music in early childhood centres was provided by the influence of the Reggio Emilia early childhood programmes. These programmes are arts based and have been of interest for Australian practitioners. For Australians influenced by Reggio Emilia it was the visual arts that were privileged and, unlike the Reggio Emilia programmes, they were mainly trained teachers who delivered these art experiences. The artists in Reggio Emilia are artists first and foremost and often not trained pedagogues. There is even a suggestion in some of the early literature that pedagogical training might distract from artistic expression (Daichendt, 2009). The notion that an artist can best deliver the expressive arts in an early childhood centre, rather than a teacher, became a contested topic. The idea that art teachers should be able to do what they teach is supported in the centre where this research was based. There is a policy of employing artists with specific expertise, teaching qualifications being less important than technical skills in the arts. In this book we introduce three music teachers who were all musicians. None had teacher training. Their different styles, musical tastes and philosophical interpretations of their music made what each brought to the setting unique. The fourth protagonist described was a home-room teacher with a love of music and a family background of singing and performance.

The centre that hosted this research is attached to a university, has a strong research culture and has an arts-based programme that has been influenced by ideas of Child Art, the progressive education movement, emergent curriculum and the Reggio Emilia programmes. The centre has employed many artists over the years with expertise including drama, dance, painting, literature, clay and music. The chapters in this book explore the research that involved the children and their music. The three musicians and their work are described and a number of the projects the children embarked upon discussed. Arising from the two drivers of this research are questions about children's competence when presented with aesthetic and complex materials to explore (Chapter 3), the impact of adults and children experiencing music as a community endeavour (Chapter 4), an extended journey into the world of the fairy tale through Mozart's *The Magic Flute* (Chapter 5), a qualified early childhood teacher supporting the music and musicians, through 'intentional teaching' (Epstein, 2005), which included an unusual collaborative effort that involved the whole centre (Chapter 6). Chapter 1 provides context for the book, Chapter 2 examines ideas underpinning an early childhood arts education programme and describes the centre where the musical events took place, the theoretical foundations of the approach to arts and early childhood education and some historical detail on how these practices emerged. The third chapter starts to give examples of the work of the musicians and the children. The book is structured into three parts: Part I is the theoretical overview; Part II is about the children, the musicians and the music; Part III revisits the research through the eyes of one of the main protagonists, as well as looking to the future.

This research was carried out in a national context where there has been a reduction of music and the arts generally. This is a phenomenon that has been reflected in early childhood teacher education programmes in many countries.

As images of children increasingly focus on future lives as skilled workers in the global knowledge economy, the early childhood curriculum increasingly emphasises formal literacy and numeracy learning over other languages of childhood, such as music. We believe music, in all its forms, is a culturally significant activity, and is associated with a number of the 100 languages of the child (Edwards, Gandini and Forman, 1998) and is the right of a child, in a society like Australia, where music, as an expressive activity, is present in myriad permutations. In a diverse, multicultural society it provides a medium for meaningful exchange across different population groups. This book presents research findings that:

- Reaffirm children's communicative competence when exposed to high-quality musical experiences
- Provide new perspectives on children's ability to engage with music in many diverse forms
- Explore and promote the role of the musician as artist/teacher
- Support an argument that the arts are an important part of human experience and should be accorded citizenship rights in early childhood programmes.

In this introductory background chapter, we therefore discuss the role of music in early childhood education and care programmes, the importance of music in children's programmes, historical influences in Australia and comment on the research that has focused on young children and music. This background has international relevance as Australia was subject to many of the same ideas influencing early childhood practice and theory, across the twentieth century, as many other countries. The research centre where these studies took place was established in the early 1990s and was, therefore, a part of the flowering of early thought that came to the fore at that time. Katz and Chard (2000) had felt the need for a more intellectual approach to young children's early experiences, Jones and Nimmo (1994) were articulating the notion of the emergent curriculum, while educational thinkers like Bruner (1991) and Gardner (1990) were introducing new ideas. Into this zeitgeist came the discovery of the programmes of Reggio Emilia (Edwards, Gandini and Forman, 1998) and it was in this moment of history that this centre embarked upon a serious journey into project-based curriculum using the arts as a major vehicle. The first project to be recorded and written up in-depth was the Octopus Project. This project was heavily music based and is described in Chapter 2 as part of the background to the musical narratives detailed in Part II of the book.

The role of music in early childhood education and care programmes

Music has long been considered an important part of the early childhood programme as an expressive form to assist children in gaining a sense of self, as a cultural activity that indicates knowledge and connectedness to the wider society, as literacy and as an activity that could be emotionally satisfying. The influence of the developmental psychologists on early childhood programmes has meant that domains of development historically have been used to record observations of children's growth and development (e.g., Lightfoot, Cole and Cole, 2005). For language and communication, children's early speech patterns were observed to be prosodic and music, especially singing, to be a means to emotionally communicate with a very young child. Nursery rhymes and lullabies are examples of songs used to sooth, relax and engage in linguistic play. For those early childhood teachers of a more didactic nature, chanting and singing were considered to be important mnemonic strategies, as is instanced by such popular songs as the 'Alphabet Song' in English. Hearing is the first sense that is fully developed and it is, therefore, an important reference for the infant. Gardner suggests that because of this, music, which is based on active listening and expression, is the first of the multiple intelligences that is available to the child as a way of meaning-making and a source of pleasure: 'The single most important thing in education is for each person to find at least one thing that he/she connects to, gets excited by, feels motivated to spend more time with' (Gardner, 1981, p. 70).

Music is considered important in early childhood in a number of forms, including movement and dance, sound-making, listening and singing. Linked to the idea of kineaesthetic learning, children, through these musical activities, are combining expression with emotion, non-verbal communication and cognitive understanding when they combine theorising with intent and possibly performance. Music lends itself to Dewey's ideas about learning by 'doing' (1944). Piaget could view music as a language, sensory motor experience and symbolic play (1962). Vygotsky's theories on the role of language in development and that learning can lead development are also relevant to musical explorations (1978). Vygotsky has become a major theoretical influence on early childhood services internationally, so it is worth identifying the approach to music taken in this book – that is, as a language of childhood – and finding resonance for this idea in a Vygotskian framework. Music is an important expression of personal preference and also a reflection of the cultural setting. Music has both social and historical significance. In early childhood services, music can be viewed as a language through which children can express knowledge and interpretations of their worlds and, therefore, is central to the development of thought and consciousness. It is through internalising musical encounters shared on the physical, social and cultural plane that the child interprets experience and gains a means and form by which to express this interpretation of reality.

Theories of children and competence in this research arose from the influence of Vygotskian ideas that children's construction of meaning is contextual. Actions take place within cultural and historical contexts with other actors. Dewey argued that children will be selective and reactive to knowledge encountered. Personal tastes, desires and previous experience will influence what the child takes from the learning situation. The children described in this book are participants in musical endeavours and protagonists in their own learning. The musical experiences that the children were exposed to were of high quality and this is crucial to the competence, understanding and meaning-making displayed.

> To say that education is a social function, securing direction and development in the immature through their participation in the life of the group to which they belong, is to say that education will vary with the quality of life which prevails in the group. (Dewey, 1944, p. 81)

Vygotsky's (1962) statement that learning can lead development has changed attitudes to children and perceptions of their competence. Educationalists have suggested that this concept of Vygotsky's should be linked to Gardner's ideas about ways of seeing and preferred styles of learning (Beliavsky, 2006). For Vygotsky, language was the major cognitive tool and his views on the relationship between thought and language represent the child's development of understanding of the world and culture in two ways. Exposure to formal language provides the opportunity to learn the language of the social group; through a process of internalisation the child can use the language to think and interpret the social milieu. Therefore, the child learns about the world and others in it through social mediation and is able to creatively interpret, adapt and make meaning of experience through cognitive processes. The relationship between language and thought is summed up by the famous quote from Vygotsky: 'A word devoid of thought is a dead thing, and the thought unembodied in words remains a shadow' (1962, p. 153). In the same way, children's experimentation with musical forms and their interactions with music and more knowledgeable members of the music culture will scaffold children's musical skills, conceptual understandings and ability to use music for creative expression. In the music projects described in the chapters in this book, children are observed exploring instruments in mindful ways, showing interest in words and sounds and being able to converse using instruments to make symbols that give meaning to the exchange. These children display competence in listening, reading non-verbal language, a sense of the dramatic and use of duration and many other elements important for musical communication as they engage in musical play and activity.

Changes in technology have brought about important developments for children and music. In recent years, digital technology has become an important literacy that has the potential to enhance the connection between the home and the early childhood centre. Conversations about how to use digital technology are not new, but what has happened is that many unintentional benefits have occurred. In the research discussed in this book, we report on various uses of technology within the centre and examples of home use of media that added to the centre experiences of the children. In the past, music education has been framed by an approach to curriculum and pedagogy passed down from previous generations, but now technology has helped remove the distance between music in early childhood services and children's musical cultures and contexts (Young, 2009). Research on young children and music increasingly reveals new connections between home and community as children have increased access to digital musical commodities (Lum, 2008; Young, 2009). The following anecdote, further explored in Chapter 5, is an example of one of these connections.

A group of children was preparing to watch the film of *The Magic Flute* (Taymor, 2010). The first week of the film had been a preparation for the opera and the opening scenes had shown actors making up and discussing roles. The children wanted to see more of 'the movie' and it was decided to play it as a serial at the end of their formal music session each week. In the second week of the serialised opera film, the music teacher was cautioning the children that some of the costumes might be frightening. The opening scenes feature a 'scary serpent'. One child tells the others, 'Don't worry, my grandpa and I watch this bit on YouTube; it's a bit scary at first but it is just a story.'

Influences in Australian early childhood music education

Music is part of the culture of societies all over the world and young children have the right to experience playful music activities from infancy, not only for the positive contribution music can make to development and formal literacy and numeracy learning, but also as a foundation for later pleasurable participation in this expressive art form.

In Australian early childhood centres, in the 20th century, two major influences on music experiences for young children were Dalcroze (Pope, 2008) and Kodaly (Hoermann and Bridges, 1989). The early childhood community in Australia welcomed the musical philosophies of Kodaly and Dalcroze. While Dalcroze was popular in the early part of the century, it was the physical educators who first showed an interest in his ideas. The influence of Dalcroze was followed by an interest in Kodaly; the latter's approach became part of the Hungarian music curriculum in 1945 and by the 1960s had a strong following in Australia. From Kodaly came the idea that music and music education is a right of all children, and from Dalcroze came notions of the importance of the mind and body in harmony. These were attractive concepts during times when the world had experienced turmoil. Dalcroze and ideas of personal peace and physical harmony were attractive during and after the First World War; Kodaly's approach became popular after the Second World War, with an emphasis on all children, connectedness to their own culture and children as possessors of rights.

A major enthusiast for Dalcroze, influential in Australian early childhood circles, was Heather Gell. Gell was introduced to the principles of eurhythmics at the Kindergarten Teacher's College in Adelaide between the years 1915 and 1918. By 1924 she was teaching eurhythmics to early childhood pre-service teachers, a national organisation had been established and she was involved in radio and early television programmes as producer and consultant. Her major publication, *Music, Movement and the Young Child* (Gell, 1949), was widely used in teacher education and was translated into Japanese in 1958. Another Japanese edition appeared in 1978. Gell was involved in the radio show, *Music through Movement*, which was produced by the Australian Broadcasting Commission (ABC) from 1938 to 1965. By the 1970s, however, fewer pre-service early childhood teachers had a strong music education background and Gell's musical arrangements were beyond many of the students studying to become teachers.

While the influence of Dalcroze has declined, Kodaly has remained popular partly as a result of a children's song book, produced by Deanna Hoermann and Doreen Bridges, called *Catch a Song* (1989). This book became a major text for students studying in early childhood programmes at university and technical college and is still used in many services today. Designed for use in early childhood programmes, each song is accompanied by teaching notes on the musical element illustrated in the song and suggested activities to introduce to children. Many of the melodies are Hungarian, though words considered culturally suitable for young Australians have been added – for example, the song 'Kangaroo' (p. 91) is a Hungarian song and the words have been changed for the Australian context. For each song in the book, the melody is expressed as a single line on the treble clef, chords are provided and two commercial recordings of all the songs were released simultaneously. Of the three musicians described in the chapters in this book, two used material from *Catch a Song*. Leah, in Chapter 3, used a mixture of Kodaly, Steiner and other material, while Kylie (Chapter 5) was heavily influenced by Kodaly, trained in the Kodaly method and used Kodaly elements to shape her approach to teaching music to the children. Singing was emphasised and these two musicians also used versions of the tonic *solfa* when singing with the children.

Some specialist music teachers in Australia did experience some conflict with the Kodaly method, while generally approving the principles. De Vries (2001), in an article discussing his own childhood experiences and then his teaching experiences in Queensland, where Kodaly was adopted into the music curriculum, made this comment:

> Living and working in Australia, one would assume Australian folk songs (folk music of the mother tongue, as advocated by Kodaly) would be part of the music program, but this is not the case in the Queensland Music Program because many Australian folk songs are diatonic, begin with an anacrusis, and are in 6/8 or 3/4 meter. Judy Johnson explains that such songs are considered unsuitable for skill acquisition in the initial stages of a Kodaly-based program. … As a result, English, Hungarian, and Irish folk-song material predominates. These songs are useful for teaching specific musical skills, such as simple sol-fa, time names, and in-tune singing development (p. 24).

Although music remained part of the daily programme in early childhood services, the rapid increase of childcare centres saw different types of training introduced for those who would work with children from birth to five years. Formal music had been an essential component of early childhood teacher training. Bridges comments:

> For example, [the writer], in charge of music at the Sydney NSTC from 1974–78, had one full-time and two part-time assistants for a total of about 230 students. Music (with movement) was taught to all students (mostly in

tutorial groups) in all three years of the course, for a total of over 100 hours, plus electives (including lessons in piano or guitar) for second and third year students. (Bridges, 2008, p. 10)

New centres however, built in the 1970s no longer considered a piano to be a compulsory part of the furniture. Tape recorders were cheap, portable and recorded children's music was freely available with a growing number of musicians producing albums targeted at young children – for example, Peter Combe and Franciscus Henri. This change was reflected in teacher education courses. The arts in university teacher programmes were often presented in an integrated fashion, or two or three arts were covered as 'representatives' of all art forms. Arts courses were variously presented as 'creative arts', 'expressive arts', 'performing arts', or simply 'arts'.

The type of music being sung, danced to, or listened to was also changing. Music texts had often been didactic (e.g., Champion de Crespigny, 1958) and designed to assist teachers in planning their daily music sessions. These were often formulaic. Mary Champion de Crespigny had been involved with *Music for Movement* (ABC) and later *Playschool* (ABC); she released a number of albums of children's songs and musical arrangements with sample lesson plans for early childhood teachers (Champion de Crespigny, 1958). Each plan was made up of a list of equipment needed and the activity was divided into four parts, which consisted of a warm-up, movement exercises, the musical point being explored and the last part of the music session, allowing for creative use of the musical element that had been introduced. One such lesson had the aim of helping the children respond to basic rhythms. The material needed was a drum and a picture of 'See-saw Marjory Daw'. The drum was used for the warm-up as children were encouraged to gallop freely to the beat while songs in 6/8 time were played. 'A good presentation of a lesson need not depend solely on the teacher's pianistic ability, as the whole range of percussion instruments can be explored, and movement with singing is to be encouraged' (Champion de Crespigny, 1958, p. 3).

The second part of the lesson plan contrasted the galloping with swaying to selected songs, most of which were in 3/4 time, with an exception being 'See-saw Marjory Daw'. The third activity in the lesson involved the children walking, running and skipping to the same tune, 'Twinkle Twinkle Little Star', played in common time for the walking and running, with the running version containing nearly all semi-quavers; the skipping version was played in 6/8 time. The sheet music was available for all three iterations of the song, with other variations added for differing responses – for example, repeating an octave higher for running on toes. 'Twinkle Twinkle Little Star' was one of a group of songs called 'utility tunes' (p. 25). In the last part of the lesson, children returned to the song 'See-saw Marjory Daw', looked at the picture, discussed different ways of making see-saws in music and were encouraged to 'skip freely' and then make see-saws. This section of the lesson was referred to as 'creative' (p. 3).

This lesson plan reminds one of the authors of this book of her training and early teaching days. For many years the idea that children's group times should have a core concept that would be embedded in the third activity introduced to the children was taught at universities and tertiary colleges; the above plan for a music group is a prime example. The details of the plan provided here can be compared with the examples of music plans prepared by the musicians, described in this book, which have been presented in later chapters.

As time spent studying music in pre-service teacher courses declined, approaches to presenting music to children and the necessity to have specific skills also decreased. Other major music influences for teachers and children came through radio and, increasingly, television. In 1966, the television show *Playschool* (ABC), based on a show in the UK with the same name, commenced. Although based on the UK production, the Australian series of *Playschool* has probably become one of the most influential expressions of Australian children's culture. Music was a major part of this expression. Between 1976 and 2011 no fewer than seventeen albums were produced. Another mainstay for parents and early childhood teachers alike was *The Useful Book: Songs and Ideas from Playschool* (Clarke, 1994) and *The New Useful Book: Songs and Ideas from Playschool* (Clarke, 2003). The emphasis is now moving to availability of music and ideas through an increasingly accessible media. This has occurred as kindergarten training colleges have been subsumed into universities or technical colleges and music, once a specialist area of practice, is increasingly taught by generalist pedagogues. Time allocation for the study of music has decreased as regulatory and quality improvement requirements dominate a busy curriculum. The introduction of early childhood curriculum, or frameworks, has been instrumental in making the idea of music one that should belong in the everyday. This has the potential to bring about fundamental change.

The children who were part of this research attend an Australian early childhood setting, but the context is similar to early childhood settings in many countries. As governments pay increased attention to the importance of the early years (OECD, 2006), the idea of creating a common language for early childhood educators, through frameworks based on learning outcomes, has become a common government practice. Australia has followed this path and it is interesting to study the presence of music in the document *Belonging, Being and Becoming: Early Years Learning Framework for Australia (EYLF)* (DEEWR, 2009). This learning framework is the first national curriculum in early childhood that Australia has produced; its meanings and implementation have been discussed widely in the sector. The *EYLF* has five learning outcomes and music is first mentioned in outcome three, which is 'Children have a strong sense of wellbeing' and are seen as taking 'increasing responsibility for their own health and physical wellbeing' (DEEWR, 2009, p. 32); one way to achieve this is to 'respond through movement to traditional and contemporary music, dance and storytelling' (DEEWR, 2009, p. 32). In outcome five, 'Children are effective communicators', music is referred to in the preamble as an important expressive medium that leads to social connectedness and also as a form of literacy. Examples are given of how this might be achieved if children: 'use language and representations from play, music and art to share and project meaning' (DEEWR, 2009, p. 42); 'use the creative arts such as drawing, painting, sculpture, drama, dance, movement, music and storytelling to express ideas and make meaning' (DEEWR, 2009, p. 40). Educators should 'provide a range of resources that enable children to express meaning using visual arts, dance, drama and music' (DEEWR, 2009, p. 42).

This approach to music suggests change has occurred in how music is seen. Music is no longer a discrete activity but part of children's ways of exploring and understanding meaning, belonging across the day in many spontaneous events. This broadening of the view of music, expressed in the *EYLF* above, is reflected in new music subjects being developed for early childhood pre-service teachers. One author of this book has recently been given *carte blanche* to develop a stand-alone music course for pre-service teachers. This has not happened at her university for decades. However, although skills and technique are still important, the subject guide also reflects the approach taken in the new curriculum:

> You will be able to support active learning approaches to early childhood music education and plan formal and informal music and movement experiences for children. Emphasis will be on music across the day and as a support for children to develop language and physical competence and extend their understanding of a variety of cultures and styles of communication. (Acker, 2014)

De Vries (2013) and others have noted how music manifests in early childhood programmes and how this has changed. They suggest access to digital technology has altered children's knowledge and experience. They identify teachers as less likely to adopt some of the newer technologies. In the chapters in this book we report on the use of technologies by the centre staff, the children, the families and the musicians. We have observed technology in the context of tool use and not as a trick of the trade. Our experience suggests that educators and, in this case, musicians, applied the use of technology when it enhanced or enabled particular activities and it was valuable in connecting children's experiences across contexts. In the next section of this introductory chapter we present a brief review of some of the research literature we have drawn on to interpret young children's activities with music.

Music research

Studying young children and music is not a new occupation. From the time of Plato, the question of the role of music in human experience has interested educators (Bridges, 2008). Musical activities, often with an emphasis on singing, have been researched. Singing is an occupation that can be undertaken spontaneously (Barrett, 2006) and also in more structured events like planned groups (Acker, 2010). Singing has been linked to language, cognitive and social development (Dunbar-Hall, 1984; Kalmar, 1989; Acker, 2008). Children's musical expression has been the focus of research and children's own interpretations of musical conventions has been a long-term interest (Moorhead and Pond, 1978). Researchers continued to extend this type of research into the home (Moog, 1976). Bayless and Ramsey (1987) described the many ways that children could use music for imaginative expression, to reflect thoughts and feelings and for drama. By three, they have an understanding of concepts like pitch, dynamics, tempo and duration and can use these to deliver memorised songs or for music, spontaneous singing or instrumentals that they compose themselves.

In recent years, early childhood music research has become more inclusive of all early childhood programmes. This is significant as more children worldwide are in out-of-home settings in the years before school and these settings take myriad forms. This has also created opportunities to observe children in many different situations. Some of the topics researchers have focused on include children's musical activities in diverse settings (Suthers, 2004), the role of educators, early childhood training (Morin, 2001) and professional development (de Vries, 2013; Suthers, 2004), home/family connections (de Vries, 2009; Lum, 2008; McPake, Plowman and Stephen, 2012), the impact of specialised music programmes (Hanna, 2013), children's competence (Nyland, Ferris and Deans, 2005), music versus the visual in arts provision (Barrett, 1993) and the influence and role of new technologies (McPake, Plowman and Stephen, 2012; Young, 2008, 2009).

Some researchers have focused on the confidence with which teachers tackle music with the children in their childcare centres and pre-schools. In her doctoral study, Suthers (2004) investigated the music experiences offered to toddlers in a childcare centre. Using participatory observation, a year-long music programme was provided that explored the efficacy of using music to support the programme at particular times of the day. These were: routines, free play and group times. Suthers found that many of the early childhood-trained professionals were capable of using music with, and for, young children but felt that a lack of confidence was a major constraint. Other participant observation studies have included introducing multicultural experiences to children (Acker, 2010), designing and running music sessions for educators and, finally, exploring the use of CDs (de Vries, 2013). In collaboration with early childhood staff, de Vries provided and observed music experiences within the early childhood programme. He found staff lacked confidence and recommended the use of prerecorded music for singing, if needed, and also encouraged formal music groups. Downie (2003), as a teacher-researcher with specialised musical skills, used a narrative approach to record her experience of providing music education in early childhood settings.

The development of formal resources to support teachers to include music when working with children has grown exponentially. Hands and Martin (2003) researched the impact of a 'fundamental movement skills' resource; the results were reported from the teacher's perspective and the child's perspective in two separate papers jointly published. Gillespie and Glider (2010) found that children's spontaneous music-making across the day was not noticed and music mainly consisted of didactic songs to support other areas of the early childhood curriculum, such as mathematical concepts, or CDs to encourage co-operation during routines. Many resources available promote music as a way to teach about specific areas of the programme and there is an abundance of DVDs, books, CDs and YouTube clips giving examples of songs to sing to enhance the understanding – for example, of maths and literacy concepts. In the projects described in this book, technology was often utilised purposively to support musical explorations.

Important research for the project described here was that which examined children's competence to respond to and engage in a variety of sophisticated musical experiences. Adults often found that children's competence, understanding and ability to theorise on the material available exceeded adults' expectations. In a project enacted in the centre where this research took place, Deans, Brown and Dilkes (2005) designed a study to research children's awareness and explorations of sound in their immediate environment. They found that the children were sensitive to and articulate about this aspect of their surroundings. Children explored the sounds of their natural environment, including a nearby river and bushland. The centre and children, as a physical and social focus, are described in Chapter 2. Tafuri's (2008) work with mothers and babies was a detailed study of how exposure can assist development. Children's use of music as an indication of creative engagement has been observed (Barrett, 2006). The significance of the social context in which a child developed musical understanding and skills was noted by de Vries (2004).

Suthers (2004) explored children's use of language to label musical experiences. In interviews, she found children used the word 'music' as a way to describe their activity (such as dance, singing, instrument playing), instead of using the name of the activity. When asked to name a combination of different musical activities, some said 'games'. She speculates that a concept of music is more likely to develop when children are encouraged to be music-makers, actively exploring the elements of music for themselves, in order to develop a music vocabulary.

Another focus of research has been a tension in regard to the place of arts in early childhood. Part of this discourse has been the observation that the visual arts seem to be part of the daily life of early childhood education settings whereas music has been relegated to receive more limited attention. Barrett (1993, 2005) has queried why this is the case. This conversation about the arts is of interest for this research, as is the discussion of the relationship between children and an adult with specialist skills (de Vries, 2004; Downie, 2003). This is central to the influence that ideas of emergent curriculum in the Reggio Emilia approach has had on the research context, described in Chapters 2 and 3. Much of the Reggio Emilia literature has tended to focus on the visual arts, though there are some examples of the inclusion of music (Page Smith, 2011). Hanna (2013) has noted the dominance of the visual arts and explored the idea of using the *atelier* (studio) of the Reggio Emilia approach to include of music. Describing the *atelierista* (the artist in the studio) as a facilitator who provides materials for artistic exploration, she suggests that: 'teachers who are already familiar with art materials and processes have a pre-established mental framework in artistic expression that could be expanded to include the musical arts' (n.p.).

Following this theme of the *atelierista*, Nieuwmeijer (2013) explored the impact of musicians working with children and the effects that could be achieved when musicians and teachers worked collaboratively to provide musical experiences for children. This is a theme of Chapter 7, where we discuss the role of a teacher who enthusiastically bridged the music experiences the children enjoyed with the musician by expanding the ideas and theories, through provocations in her own teaching and learning environment. Bond (2013) also researched Reggio Emilia principles of practice to highlight what music educators might take from this approach.

Though some music-making activities have not changed, there is now an abundance of 'educational' commercial products sold to parents. Among these is an increasing number of digital musical merchandise available for young children (Hughes, 2005). Once these wares consisted mainly of CDs, DVDs or musical toys, but, more recently, tablets have become popular and some researchers suggest these may have learning potential that goes beyond what children can do during spontaneous play. Children are now frequently exposed to digitally produced music rather than traditional instrumentation. This is a significant change in children's musical experience as digitally produced music sounds are environmentally prevalent just about everywhere. The digital age influences what children bring to their early childhood setting, what is possible for them to encounter there and, as evidenced in the earlier anecdote regarding the child watching YouTube with her grandfather, there is a possibility of extended connections being made.

An important influence on our research has been the growing interest in technology and music over the years. As technologies become more available in early childhood settings and children's homes, it has been interesting to observe the purposeful use of technologies to support the musical explorations the children in this research were involved in. A recurring comment about teachers and technology and the need for professional development in the use of digital technologies with young children has appeared in the literature (de Vries, 2013). There are assumptions that many educators, both generalists and music educators, may not understand, or be willing to utilise, digital technologies (Yelland, 2011). As digital technology has become such a presence in everyone's lives, we have drawn upon the research we have conducted to observe and interpret the role that technology plays in these particular musical events and report on this throughout the book, surmising how this will influence future practice.

Conclusions

In this book we argue that music is a valuable expression of culture and that all children have a right to high-quality music experiences. The centre where the children's musical activities were observed used an emergent curriculum model and the early childhood programmes of Reggio Emilia, with the concept of the 100 languages of childhood as an exemplar when focusing on the arts. Emphasis has been on project-based practice and this theme is explored in Chapter 2. An issue we take up is that the Reggio Emilia approach is premised on the idea of the 100 languages, but the languages that have been associated with these programmes have been quite limited. Visual arts and crafts and the aesthetics of the constructed environment have been most in evidence. We are hopeful, with recent reform agendas that have seen the introduction of early childhood frameworks and an emphasis on a broader more integrated curriculum, that it is timely to advocate for music to also have a prominent place in the languages of childhood. As Barrett (2005, p. 261) has said: 'Music is a powerful yet poorly understood force in children's early development and identity construction.'

This book

The story in this book is presented in three sections. The first two chapters provide context. This first chapter has outlined some theoretical and practical aspects of early childhood programmes, music and young children, with some historical background included to give a foundation for some of the material discussed. This contextual view is supported by the second chapter, which is a detailed description of the research site, the physical, cultural and social setting for the music activities undertaken. The second section, Chapters 3–7, are accounts of each of the musicians who participated in the research and a chapter on one of the educators who was a major protagonist in supporting music in the centre and the story of the choir that grew as a child-initiated group as a result of the music experienced. The last part of the book goes more deeply into some of these experiences to bring them together, find connections and adopt another lens through which to view the events described. Chapter 8 presents an in-depth view of some of the children and the learning that they experienced during the time the research took place. These stories are presented in the format of 'learning stories'. Individual children's approaches to the music, their own understandings and their creative expression emerge in this chapter. To conclude the book, we have examined the emerging themes that have been identified and revisited these with the director of the programme. The director has been with the programme for twenty years and can be regarded as the author of the arts programme. She and the researchers have worked together throughout the project from the time the first musician was employed. The director's insights and the themes from the different stories are brought together to conclude the narrative.

2

EARLY CHILDHOOD ARTS EDUCATION

A case study

Introduction

This chapter explores the arts programme in a particular early childhood centre. The centre was the context in which the research reported in this book took place over a ten-year period. The particular characteristics of the centre have been described here, as these have a bearing on how the programme has evolved. This involves an explanation of the centre's educational, physical, social and cultural environment. An understanding of the views, values, philosophical and theoretical approaches towards the arts, early childhood education and the way these two domains might interact to inform curriculum are crucial, since they were drivers in the stories told in the following chapters. This is the story of one centre, and is not intended to be representative of the usual practice in the sector, but is presented, rather, as documentation and an exploration of how this interplay emerged in this particular setting. The role of research in the development of these issues in the centre's programme is discussed, along with the centre's position in the international discourse regarding arts-based early childhood education.

The environment

The environment in which a centre operates is significant, and has an important influence on the way a centre evolves. Even those aspects which are immutable, such as the geographical location and the social and cultural backgrounds of the families from which the children are drawn, lend themselves to being considered as background on which the centre can draw in a constructive and creative way. Other aspects of the environment are open to being deliberately crafted and developed according to the values, philosophy and theoretical standpoints of the centre.

In addition, the serendipitous, unplanned elements of individual style and person-alities may also influence the nature and delivery of content and the context itself.

The centre catered for 160 children aged three to five years. As an extended-hours pre-school, children attended for a full day, from 8.30 am until 5.30 pm, either five days a week, or, as part-time participants, for two or three days a week. Children were grouped into 'home-rooms' based on age, working with two quali-fied early childhood educators. Home-rooms were given names of Australian flora: Eucalypts; Waratahs; Banksia; Blue Gums and Wattles. Significantly for the narra-tives unpacked in this book, the ELC was established as a research centre attached to a major university, directed by a senior academic from the faculty of education. As such, the university had expectations that the staff would be actively involved in reflective research projects, such as those described in this book, which would have an impact on the centre's curriculum, add to scholarly discourse in the field of early childhood education and inform work within the university's early childhood edu-cation courses. Parents enrolled their children in the programme understanding this research context and, indeed, many appreciated the potential educational advan-tages of this kind of setting and were pleased to be involved (Deans and Brown, 2008). The academic framework meant that this centre was unusual compared to many mainstream centres as it had considerable resources available through the relationship with the university. The physical building and surrounds had a history entwined in the local community and considerable early childhood expertise was available to support research projects.

The centre is located in an inner suburb of Melbourne, close to the city's major river and the natural bush parklands adjacent to it. It is next to a children's farm located on the oldest tract of land in the city continuously farmed since white set-tlement. It is also next to a convent and its gardens, a historical complex established in 1865 by the Roman Catholic Order of the Sisters of the Good Shepherd to look after the city's destitute women, but now a vibrant community precinct, home to practising artists and a community fine-music broadcaster. These physical and his-torical contexts were tangible and formed a unique and interesting setting for the centre and its work.

The ELC was housed in what was the parochial primary school, attached to the convent of the Sisters of the Good Shepherd, an old red brick school building con-structed in the heyday of primary school education in the early twentieth century. While the old school had been renovated and adapted to suit the current early childhood education purpose, the building retained much of its historic appearance. The garden, once a bitumen desert, had been redesigned to suit young children's play activities, offering a well-tended and attractive setting for outdoor programmes. Among the bushes and other plants was a judiciously placed wooden amphitheatre in the garden which had been designed to encourage dramatic play, including musical play and improvisation. This was an area where children could play alone, in small groups or invite an adult to join in. Musical instruments such as drums, bells, tambourines, marimbas and large xylophones were frequently placed in the amphitheatre for the children's spontaneous use.

As the visitor entered the ELC it was clear that this was an environment which had been deliberately constructed to enhance a particular view of early childhood growth and learning. A hallway ran along the inner side of the L-shaped building, with direct access to children's home-rooms and the garden playground via a wide, covered veranda area. This space was immediately engaging. Glass cases, at a child's eye-level, displayed some of the children's ceramic work. For example, while the centre was involved in a project about Antarctica, ceramic penguins that the children had constructed were displayed; on another wall children's drawings and paintings of the pale, transparent and icy landscape of Antarctica, with their stories attached, illustrated the ideas and concepts in which the art works were embedded. On another section of the wall, weekly displays of the curriculum plans and session reports from the centre's arts programme in visual art, drama, music and story creation reported on current curriculum planning and activities.

The hallway was busy with children as the home-rooms opened from this space. This corridor was often crowded with children moving to and from the gallery space used for music, and to and from the veranda and the playground. Adults, teachers, parents, visitors and administrative staff also used the passage, and recognised its function as a space designed not only to communicate information about the programme and the life of the centre's community, but also to engage the senses and to present a window into the place the arts held in the centre's views about early children and their education. The space gave the opportunity for the children to offer art works as gifts to the community in the tradition of the Reggio Emilia educational approach. This practice is discussed below. The impression was that, while this was a busy space in the active life of the centre, deliberate care was taken to ensure that this was an engaging and aesthetically pleasing space. This was possibly the largest space in the centre, being approximately 10–12 feet wide, with well-proportioned windows and a 15-foot ceiling; it ran the full length of the main building. By the early twentieth century, the ventilated corridor had become an architectural feature in most schools; these were spaces that 'facilitated the easy distribution of people' (Jarmozek, 2010, p. 764) and came to be considered an important space for socialisation across groups while giving a wider choice for individual use of space. The corridor in the ELC was carefully designed to meet the historical purposes of such a space and was also a major communicative area. The Edwardian school corridor resembled, in daily use, the *piazza* of the pre-schools of Reggio Emilia (Edwards, Gandini and Forman, 1998).

A room more formally dedicated to the arts also opened off the passage. This was a children's art gallery, called the *Boorai*, the word for 'baby' or 'child' in the language of the Aboriginal Wurundjeri people, acknowledging that the centre was situated on land long inhabited by the Wurundjeri people before white settlement. According to the centre's description of the gallery and its function, the *Boorai* provided a:

permanent venue for the display and appreciation of children's art and stories. This unique space presents local, national and international exhibitions that stimulate and challenge audiences to recognise and value the personal and sociocultural comments expressed by children through their art and stories. These symbolic representations and related documentation, support research activity and provide teachers and parents with further understanding of the ideas, beliefs and abilities of young children (Early Learning Centre, 2014).

The centre invites other early childhood educators to contribute to exhibitions in the gallery, aims to host touring exhibitions and to develop joint exhibitions based on diverse cultural perspectives. The *Boorai* gallery was permanent, in a light, uncluttered room incorporated in the centre's building. The room had children's art displayed with respect, thoughtfully framed and hung in the style of an adult gallery. While resembling the nature of a formal art gallery as understood in the adult community, this space was also visited regularly by all members of the centre's community for other day-to-day activities, such as gatherings of all children for assemblies and, significantly for this book, as the space for specialist music sessions and performances. The room had been adapted for music activities with the addition of sound baffles, and was furnished with a white upright piano and cupboards for music instruments. The gallery space consequently formed a very particular aesthetic background for music activities.

The history of this space is worth noting. The director recollected:

> That was a bathroom when I first came here. There were five toilets and a urinal in there, and there was a wall right down the middle ... So we had toilet time, and it was written up in timetable. The urinal wasn't working – it was where the cleaner kept all the buckets. And there was a sink and there were hooks all on the wall and little face washers for towels. It was a really, really old-fashioned idea of kindergarten in the 1950s. So when the university agreed to renovation ... I said we would have to do something about the bathrooms. That's when I said we will have a multipurpose room and we will turn this into a specialised space. That was part of the vision, it was part of the vision for an artistic environment and that it was going to be a gallery was an attractive idea to the funding people. I knew the space would be great for dance and music. (Interview, 29 May 2014)

Tishman (2008) points out that museums are inevitably designs for learning. Objects, materials, art works and texts are chosen and presented and necessarily represent a view about what is on display. A visitor who is challenged by a display will be involved in active learning as a result of the experience and, given that visitors are invited to peruse as they choose, they will be employing 'personal agency'. To the extent that both the corridor and the *Boorai* space were deliberately designed and the displays selected, visitors to the space were able to interact with the available text, explanations, illustrations and art works. Therefore, the space reflected the kind of thinking more typical of a museum or gallery. While it is fair to say that many early childhood education centres display both information about their programme and aspects of the children's work, the quality of the design in this instance and the deliberate intentions for both areas were at a higher level than usual. This clearly indicated the importance to the centre staff of communicating the centre's philosophy and approaches to young children's learning. This communication, particularly regarding the role played by the arts, was a significant aspect of the programme. The presence of staff members with specific expertise in the centre, who had the skills to prepare and mount work at this level, was an important consideration.

The displays reflected a respect for children's work and, over the years since the centre was established in 1990, indicated the evolution of philosophical and theoretical views. As a research centre of the university's education faculty, the centre had ensured that its understanding of how theory informs practice was evident in its curriculum, and that this relationship was one that developed as a result of the staff being involved in reflective practice. The nub of this approach was in accordance with Deans and Brown's (2008) views of how diverse theories may produce a patchwork of partial truths. This enabled educators to review their practices.

As the displays in the passageway and the *Boorai* gallery suggested, the role of the arts in the lives of children and in early childhood education were a central focus of a long-term research interest (Deans and Brown, 2008, p. 2). Aspects of the research included the changing image of the child and the nature of the arts as symbolic languages in the context of the emergent curriculum, the role of the adult artist/teacher and the ways in which social/cultural values influence arts pedagogy and practice. The research process had, therefore, prompted a shifting, or evolutionary approach, to the arts in the programme.

As discussed in Chapter 1, historically arts education in Australia was seen as an aspect of individual, free expression; indeed, the arts in the curriculum were often referred to as the 'expressive' arts. This view of the arts, however, was not sufficiently rich to accommodate more recent theoretical work regarding how children learn, or, in sociocultural terms, regarding the significance of the environment on a child's learning. In the early days of the centre, arts practice was influenced by the prevailing assumptions in early childhood education that appropriate practice for each child should be informed by well-recognised developmental stages, a notion that did not allow for differences in social or cultural influences on the environment in which learning occurred, nor did it adequately account for differences from child to child. Teachers also were influenced by longstanding arts education theories promulgated in Australian teacher education by visual arts educators such as Herbert Read (Read, 1967) and, in early childhood, Frances Derham (1976). Derham, strongly influenced by Victor Lowenfeld (1947), encouraged activities that allowed children to explore and play with art materials. This exploration was largely without direct adult intervention. Such an approach was considered one that would encourage children to reach their creative or expressive potential, all within the confines of developmental expectations (Director, interview, 11 May 2005).

When the centre was established in 1990, the research culture and reflective practices led to challenges of established views, particularly around the growing discourse of developmentally appropriate practice (Fleer, 1995). As mentioned in Chapter 1, a range of theories were attracting attention at this time: socio-constructivist theories developed by Vygotsky (1978) were being revisited, along with such notions as the emergent curriculum explored by Jones and Nimmo (1994) and a revisiting of Dewey's project approach (Katz and Chard, 1989). The initiative coming from the Reggio Emilia pre-schools in Italy was particularly significant as this philosophy contained aspects of all the above ideas packaged into an attractive approach. Reggio Emilia provided a landscape to explore in a research context. The teacher as researcher was a new concept in constructing the role of the adult in early childhood education. The director, with a commitment to the arts, was influenced by and part of this movement.

The centre was part of this growing conversation regarding the child as com-municative and competent, now viewed as having agency and rights in their own learning within a reciprocal social environment. With learning considered to be socially constructed and generated through negotiation, according to the child's interests, staff at the centre became increasingly interested in the work of education scholars like Gardner (1983). Gardner's theories of 'multiple intelligences' became a framework suggesting that children could interpret their world through multiple 'modes', including modes specifically relevant to the arts. Music, recognised as a specific intelligence by Gardner, could now also be seen as a language of child-hood. The concept of language was expanded to include symbol systems associated with the arts, through which children could construct their world view and com-municate about their experience as participants in their culture (Bruner, 1991). These theories all offered the centre a strong validity for the place of the arts in early childhood education, and suggested a rich potential for research and reflective practices.

The project approach: an exploration of partial truths in theoretical approaches

Against the background of theories that shifted the focus for early childhood edu-cation in the early 1990s, the centre embarked on a research project in 1995 designed to explore new perspectives. With the arts as a central component, the Octopus Project brought together a team of teachers, artists and researchers to examine the possibilities of children's multi-symbolic representation within an emergent curriculum. The key questions established for the project were how teachers interpret emergent curriculum and how children's capabilities for multi-symbolic representation might be incorporated into an emergent curriculum design. In addition, the project was designed to investigate teachers critical reflec-tion, co-operative learning in dance, children's conceptions of musical improvisa-tions, project-based learning and a child-initiated curriculum (Deans and Brown, 2008). The research used ethnographic and descriptive methods to explore the 'lived experience' (van Manen, 1991) of children and adults involved in the project. Data collected included transcripts of dyadic interactions, video recordings of the programme during semi-structured interviews and artefacts arising from the children's work.

The music component of the project involved documenting how children experienced music, how they understood their experience and what teachers might be able to select from this data to help inform curriculum (Bond and Deans, 1997). The researchers focused on children who chose music as their preferred mode of experience or who initiated musical play, within the broader context of their involvement in the centre's activities. Children were observed whenever the centre's programme offered opportunities for children to engage in music: during specialist dance sessions, as audience in events involving adults playing instruments or singing, and in spontaneous playing with instruments such as tambours, tambourines, bells and drums. In the last instance, children played in the amphitheatre, which provided for outdoor play, and on a small stage for indoor activities. Children improvised, making their own sounds, alone, in collaboration with other children or in response to other children. The data collected for the wider project included videos; those segments involving children improvising music were identified. The children were shown the video clips of their own music-making, and were interviewed as they watched themselves during these activities, or immediately afterwards. Since children at the centre were accustomed to interacting with their teachers in this research context, they were accomplished at describing what they saw and how they understood what they observed. The following extract from one interview transcript is a demonstration of this process (Bond and Deans, 1997, p. 4 I).

T   So what do you think you were doing, playing these instruments?
C   To make some music, some drama.
T   Some drama, some music ... Did you need all those drums and the tambourine to make all that music?
C   Yes ... I actually wanted to make three different sounds.
T   Three different ... sit down so we can talk and be close together ... three different sounds ... and you were making three different sounds?
C   Yes ... I was making bing (sings and gestures with hand) and bong.
T   That's two.
C   The big drum was a bit like boom. Boom, boom, boom, boom.
T   That's a lovely sound.
T   You're making that with your feet as well are you? (in response to C bouncing her feet on the ground and patting hands on her knees)

As a result of analysing nine transcripts of interviews with children, the researcher found that children were revisiting their musical experiences in various ways. For example, children restated their experience with words and gestures, representing their understanding of musical concepts such as pitch and rhythm. Children were able to make judgements about qualities of sounds, and compare and refer to other children's ideas; they started to develop theories of concepts such as song, music and sound, and were able to reflect on their own decision-making. They described ways of 'doing music', such as instrumental techniques (use of beaters, for example) and the notion of rehearsing. They used some musical terminology such as fast, slow, getting faster, normal and quiet, and they sometimes made connections between their music and other experiences in the programme such as dance, referring, for example, to 'flying', or 'a snake' and sometimes explaining the sounds as associations rather than in the abstract. Children were aware of different sensory modalities used, such as hearing and feeling, and were able to consider the ways they planned, imagined and pretended, perhaps constructing a story as a way to explain their thinking (Bond and Deans, 1997, pp. 5–8). The findings from this research suggested that the children already had a complex knowledge and understanding of music, which was not necessarily recognised in common practice. For example, the practice of activities to 'reinforce the beat' does not do justice to the subtle understandings of beat and rhythm suggested in this project. During the Octopus Project, teachers also routinely invited children to 'draw something remembered', thus involving children in reflection and narration. This became an established practice (see Chapter 3) and allowed the teachers insight into the children's responses as participants, as well as providing useful data in the research process. The children's drawings support the comments above about children's competence and became part of the documentation practices at the ELC.

In accordance with Vygotskian (1978) social-constructivist learning theory, the study indicated that the children 'were deeply engaged when learning was co-constructed with adults who used a range of scaffolding techniques to explore and revisit ideas through language, dance, drama, music and visual art' (Deans and Brown, 2008, p. 341). Of particular significance to the future nature of the centre's programmes, the Octopus Project adopted the use of artist/teachers, in line with the Reggio Emilia use of artists from the community (atelierista) (Edwards, Gandini and Forman, 1998). In this educational approach, adults with skills recognised by and relevant to the adult community are employed to work with the children to share their artistic skills, views and aesthetic understandings. Not being trained early childhood educators, these artists are not guided by the usual expectations of what children are able or not able to achieve; they are, in a sense, liberated from the constraints of prescribed frameworks. Rather than employing the laissez-faire approach adopted by practitioners informed by the belief that children should be exploring individual expressions of creativity, these artists modelled their own practice, used direct instruction and sophisticated discussions with the children, drawing on a range of culturally diverse adult skills. Deans and Brown (2008) suggested that, in this way, they 'stimulated freedom of thought, risk taking, humour and pleasure among children' (p. 341). Nevertheless, Deans and Brown suggest this more direct style of teaching was still, at times, guided by children's play and by their spontaneous art-making.

The arts now had a highly significant role in the centre's view about the way children learn, having moved from earlier views regarding developmental stages, and Derham's (1976) ideas on the nature of individual expressive and creative development using a stage approach. The arts were now recognised as symbol systems, with the artists taking a major role. The use of this approach, the arts as language, in the early 1990s was significant in several ways. Artists and trained educators now came together to collaborate in establishing a lively arts programme. In early childhood centres, it was assumed that adults working as educators with children would be trained and qualified for this purpose. Using adult artists as teachers, with no formal education training, meant that it was desirable for the trained teachers working with each group to be involved in and integrated into all aspects of the programme. This strategy of employing the 'specialist' teacher differs from the more usual scenario where the generalist teacher was not always integrated into the programme; indeed, at times in some centres, a specialist teacher can allow the home-room teacher some time free for planning. Certainly, the more usual form of specialist teaching involves a sense that the specialist has the skills that the generalist lacks, and the arts are often seen, therefore, as being the domain of the specialist. Any integration from the arts sessions and the children's day-to-day programme may become problematic. In the artist/teacher model explored by the Octopus Project, there was potential for a more integrated approach simply because the home-room teachers were present at all sessions with the children. The extent to which this potential was developed is part of the story told in this book.

Significantly, the capacity of the artists to share their own artistry, arts practice and views in collaboration with the children freed the programme from the views of what would be expected by notions of age and stage development. Instead, the children were involved with learning that was co-constructed with adults in a social environment; this was a fundamental shift in thinking about the roles of both children and adults in the education process, and accorded the arts a central role in children's learning.

In relation to the views held about the nature of the arts in childhood and in early childhood education, the centre's views shifted from considering the arts as 'solely aesthetically pleasing activities' to include 'intellectual' and 'interpretive' processes that supported holistic and multi-symbolic learning. Logically, and as a consequence, children needed to be able to interpret and use the arts symbolic systems in order to participate in and to communicate through the arts. This reflects an expanded view of literacies and language already gaining currency from the work at Reggio Emilia, as in the Malaguzzi notion (Edwards, Gandini and Forman, 1998) of the '100 languages of children'.

The ways in which the Octopus Project enabled the co-construction of knowledge through mutual and collaborative exploration of ideas and interests between the adults and children facilitated a deeper understanding of the potential of an emergent curriculum framework. Deriving from research by Jones and Nimmo (1994) into programmes inspired by Malaguzzi's work in Italy in the Reggio Emilia pre-schools, the notion that respect for and documentation of children's active learning enables the development of a curriculum based on children's strengths led to the theoretical concept of emergent curriculum. Jones explains it this way:

> The goal of emergent curriculum is to respond to every child's interests. Its practice is open ended and self-directed. It depends on teacher initiative and intrinsic motivation, and it lends itself to a play-based environment. Emergent curriculum emerges from the children, but not only from the children ... Emergent curriculum emerges from the play of children and the play of teachers. It is co-constructed by the children and the adults in the environment itself. To develop curriculum in depth, adults must notice children's questions and invent ways to extend them, document what happens, and invent more questions. The process is naturally individualised. (Jones, 2012, p. 67)

Project-based learning

As a significant outcome of the development of the emergent curriculum model, the centre started to use project-based learning drawing on the children's lived and direct experience, content negotiated between children and adults, problem-setting and problem-solving. In this way, the centre was able to develop topics that could be explored across both home-room and specialist art programmes. Deans and Brown explain the process in this way:

> The research undertaken around this practice was shaped around the three questions: how does the teacher involve all children equitably in the initiation and development of projects; how does a specialist arts program balance the needs for a sequential and planned skills-based learning with content that is responsive to children's interests and preferred learning styles and how readily does theory and practice generated in Reggio Emilia (i.e. specific social and cultural context) transfer to other early learning settings? (2008, p. 343)

From this process emerged a clear sense that children, as competent and socially confident members of the centre's community, were able to articulate interests and ideas. Indeed, this was seen as a child's right (Clark and Moss, 2005; Fleet *et al.*, 2006). If the emergent curriculum was to provide meaningful results, teachers needed to develop strong skills in listening to children, as well as diverse ways to document processes to ensure that children's views were clearly visible in the curriculum. The teachers also came to understand that the balance between skills-based learning and the need to pay attention to the children's interests was an aspect of curriculum development that required examination. Deans and Brown concluded that while there was:

> much to be learned from the experience of educators in Reggio Emilia, it was the embedding of local environment and culture in the experiences of

the children and adults in this particular Australian early learning setting that guided decisions and practices around teaching and learning. (2008, p. 343)

The initial belief that good practice would result from a theoretical tapestry of 'partial truths' was, in fact, a journey that involved the teachers as researchers in a complex process of reflection and design at a level that is, perhaps, not possible in most Australian ELCs. As a designated research centre, the ELC was privileged in terms of resources and expertise. This allowed them to actively pursue a research approach, with the path found through the available possibilities uniquely the result of the work undertaken by the teachers and the children at the centre.

The Octopus Project was an inspiration for a series of subsequent projects designed on the understandings emerging from research, linking the specific social and cultural contexts and environment of these particular children to wider community issues. Working on the assumption that children are citizens of their communities, another early project involved exploring children's understandings and responses to indigenous knowledge. This was called the Coming Closer Project. In a sphere that is sometimes examined with little regard to the complexities of both indigenous knowledge and children's ways of relating to this knowledge, the project aimed to be authentic and rich and this enterprise was certainly ambitious, interesting and a test of this style of learning.

The arts provided a rich source of learning, connection and communication. Visits to the centre by elders from the indigenous community to tell indigenous stories, both contemporary and traditional, challenged both the adults and the children's understandings of concepts such as kinship, spirituality, relationships between people and land, along with other codes of behaviour. Children responded to what they remembered through arts media – drawing 'telling', storytelling and art-making. Children responded to the 'River Story', told by George Jillimablu, indicating a range of new insights into indigenous culture, expressed through indigenous art works. The story related to the time when George was rescued by his father from a flooded river during a family fishing expedition. The children used narrative, along with a drawing, to formulate and share their individual understanding of the story. Rachel, aged five, explained her thinking from a particularly visual perspective:

> There is the didgeridoo. There is the river and in the river is the tree. George is hanging onto the tree. This is the kangaroo. It's looking to the side so you can see it and the bones. Next to the river are the dots and lines. (Deans and Brown, 2008, p. 344)

Another child responded to the drama of the story, drawing an energetic series of undulating, parallel lines to indicate the dangerous flooding river waters, with a single line emerging from the water and a dot representing George holding onto the tree. Another responded to the family and social aspects of George's tale. This project was integrated into the centre's programme and was introduced into other ELCs in Melbourne and other parts of Australia (Deans and Brown, 2008, p. 345).

Through embedding the programme content in the local environment, the ELC had developed a close relationship with the nearby river and environs. This awareness of the flora and fauna of the local area led to an interest in the growing worldwide, social and political concern with environmental issues. The centre consequently reframed its arts programmes to encompass and enable learning about, through and from their own local environment. This approach also reflected the belief that children learn within their sociocultural setting. The Glass Project was a long-running example of this strategy. The project shaped arts activities for five years, and involved collaboration between the centre and a private artist's practice, Philip Stokes Studio Glass. This relationship is discussed in Chapter 7. The intention of introducing the children to Stokes was to provide children with the chance to work with local artists. Using the United Nation's framework of international themes, designed to develop concern and informed awareness of a range of environmental issues, the collaboration led to projects inspired by the International Year of Earth Sciences (2007), the International Polar Year (2008), the International Year of Astronomy (2009), the International Year of Biodiversity (2010) and the International Year of Forests (2011).

Perhaps the most surprising of these projects involved the children in a relationship that developed with scientists working at the Casey Base in Antarctica. Bob Jones, one of the scientists at Casey Base, responded to the children by considering the questions arising from the children's research about the world of Antarctica, such as 'Do Iceberg roses grow in Antarctica?' and 'Do icebergs have a heart?' Jones took these questions to his colleagues at Casey Base, involving the adults in that isolated environment with a group of curious young children. The art works evolving from this particular project reflected the children's high level of engagement in the peculiar nature of the Antarctic environment. Their paintings reflected the transparent and specific palette of Antarctic landscapes and seascapes, the exotic nature of penguins and the mystery of icebergs. The music specialist, in response to the children's interest, composed a song about 'diamond dust', an atmospheric phenomenon in the Antarctic in which the air is full of floating specks of glittering ice. The song became a favourite in the children's song repertoire.

At a more immediate, local level, projects at the centre were designed to actively engage the children in issues such as water conservation, recycling, effects of drought, pollution and endangered species. The Water for Life Project involved the children in the environment of the local river, building on concerns about the plight of the river during a dry spell. The children had discovered first-hand the effect of drought, noticed during their walks. Children sat by the river, took photographs and recorded sounds. Teachers used the children's documentation to stimulate discussion to help formulate further investigative activities, all explored through the specialist arts programme. Children used dramatic play, songs, soundscapes and image-making to explore and communicate their understanding of their own local environment.

Another project, the Environment Workshop Project: Eco-cubby, led children to consider how wider environmental issues could shape and influence the way we all choose to live our day-to-day lives at a local level. This project involved collaboration between children, families, teachers, artist and architect, and acknowledged children's capacity to design, build and show curiosity about sustainability and the application of sustainability principles in daily life. Participants became familiar with a range of design issues, natural material options and the skills involved in building the 'eco-cubby' that emerged in pride of place in the playground at the centre. The process was documented and disseminated, and, along with scale models of the eco-cubby, was displayed in February 2010 at the Sustainable Living Festival in Melbourne (Early Learning Centre, 2014).

In each of these projects, the arts provided a powerful and fundamental means for the children and the adults working with them to explore issues related to the environment in which the centre and its community lived, at levels ranging from the local, such as the centre's playground and the nearby river, to international environment concerns and projects. The arts provided the means by which children could participate in rich and sophisticated ways in issues that exercise the minds of everyone in the community, giving them tangible citizenship rights. Using a collaborative style of working between all members of the centre's community, children's learning was firmly embedded in their environment.

In line with the centre's research brief from the university, a range of methods have been developed to disseminate the results of ongoing research. Members of the centre's staff have been involved in presentations at conferences and have published widely in academic journals. The research has provided ongoing research material for students in both undergraduate and postgraduate programmes. The experience of the centre has prompted an extensive series of teacher resources such as children's books, including children's art works, videos and DVDs, with accompanying documentation. As well, displays in the centre's passage, mentioned above, have always reflected the nature of the children's responses to the projects and the curriculum emerging from them.

Three of the authors of this book joined the centre's research journey when the exploration of projects as a means of developing curriculum was well underway. While the centre's director had undertaken research specifically around children's musical improvisations as a part of the Octopus Project, she was concerned that the ways in which music was contributing to the centre's research needed to be documented more consistently. She took the step of employing the first of the music specialists, Lesley, whose work is discussed in the next chapter, and invited two of the authors to come in as participant researchers in the specialist music programme.

Conclusions

The story of the research journey undertaken by the centre and its staff and children is significant in that it illustrates a very particular kind of early learning environment, one that has deliberately explored a range of research approaches to help develop a curriculum designed specifically to suit the children involved. While all professional early childhood educators are mindful of research and reflective practice, the requirements within this centre as a designated research centre, and the methods by which they chose to proceed, made it a unique case study worthy of discussion.

That the arts became central to the ways teachers worked with the children is a fundamental outcome of the research story. The influence of the Reggio Emilia philosophy of working with practising adult artists, rather than relying on trained educators with skills in the arts, was clearly important. The centre was able to consider how this strategy might be applied in this unique kind of setting, rather than simply following the descriptions of the Reggio Emilia approach, particularly regarding working with musicians. In the time we spent at the centre, we were able to document the work of three musicians working with the children, over consecutive years, each musician bringing a quite distinctive style, passion and set of skills. Each also offered a distinct way of relating to the children and to the centre's overall programme, including the other specialist artists. Given the historical and ongoing challenges of making skilled music provision available in early childhood settings, this circumstance was significant. The two authors initially involved in the music research came into the process with a pre-existing interest in the place of specialist music teaching in an early learning context; while acknowledging the value of both the specialised understanding of music and the ability to involve children in music in sophisticated ways, we were also interested in ways in which meaningful connections might be made between the music sessions and the rest of the children's activities at the centre. This reflects the conundrum that faces all education settings wanting to offer a worthwhile music programme while relying on educators whose musical abilities are frequently under-developed and who often, the research suggests, lack confidence (Suthers, 2004). While the ways in which the generalist educators responsible for the children's home-rooms were able or even willing to collaborate with the musicians was not entirely resolved, the ongoing process of addressing the issue was a complex source of interest and offered some possible strategies. As this was a particularly well-resourced centre, these strategies presented models that, while perhaps not entirely transferrable to other situations, nevertheless proffer some possible approaches to explore.

The use of projects as a means of developing an emergent curriculum is one approach other centres have considered, so the value of this research is to present a high-quality example that explores possibilities and challenges. The opportunities discovered by involving the whole community, with their skills, enthusiasms and knowledge, in the way children learn, along with the sense that children are rightful citizens in their community, is a powerful strategy. The capacity of the arts to carry this approach successfully is a formidable advocacy for the importance of the arts as a means of providing children with many and diverse languages with which to interact with their world.

The research described in this book involves musicians, each quite individual in their approach and whose own work with the children evolved with experience and reflection, against a background of evolving and developing curriculum approaches across the whole centre. The ELC's belief that the most constructive and interesting way forward was likely to involve drawing on a range of different theoretical approaches certainly provided a rich background for the documenting and exploration of the role of music in this setting, leading us along some unexpected paths. Our research was also, of necessity, emergent, and involved us in frequent reflection and repositioning.

In the following chapters we tell the stories of three musicians, a children's choir, one of the home-room teachers and the director's perspective. The next chapter recounts music experiences developed when the first musician, Lesley, came to the centre.

PART II
The music

3

A SEARCH FOR MEANING AND COMMUNICATIVE COMPETENCE THROUGH THE LANGUAGE OF MUSIC

Introduction

Lesley was the first musician; her introduction into the ELC's programme was somewhat serendipitous. While music had been part of the ongoing curriculum research at the centre, no specialists were specifically employed to work in this area, as there were for visual arts and designated drama sessions. The director was concerned that the skill of the generalist teachers did not represent the 'pure' skills that would allow an appropriate level of sophistication (Director, 11 May 2005). The director had discovered that one of the assistants at the centre was a musician, so the director suggested that this assistant might consider running some music sessions for the children. From this beginning, Lesley was employed to work with each group of children, the Banksias, Waratahs, Wattles, Blue-gums and Eucalypts, for a weekly, one-hour session. According to the Reggio Emilia model, she was not a trained teacher, but rather was to work with the children to share her own passion and expertise in music, in the shifting context of the centre's ongoing curriculum research.

The centre was already working with an emergent curriculum model, and was now experienced in developing projects to engage the children in a wide range of interests and issues. In particular, the environment, both immediate to the children and more widely, was actively used to inspire curriculum; the nearby river emerges as a constant theme in this book. The arts specialists were accustomed to working within the context of the centre's wider curriculum interests, and were already providing a powerful expression of the children's capacity to explore their world in sophisticated ways. The children's work was routinely displayed in the passageway for the centre's adult community; the arts were already a visible and tangible part of the centre's curriculum research journey. Lesley took on the task of finding ways for music to add to this existing culture. In this chapter we introduce Lesley, discuss her work through examples of planning and her approach to repertoire, and then present in-depth observations into three events that occurred during music sessions. We draw on interview data, documents, including copies of plans and reports from the passage, music with notes, photographs and field notes to recount the story of the first musician in the centre. We also took the role of participant observers at times.

The musician

Lesley was the oldest of five children, in a family that valued music and music education. Her story indicates a belief in music as a means of personal expression that started early in her life, one that suited her shyness as a child. She played piano by ear from the age of four (only a little older than the children involved in this study) and then formally from the age of five. In addition to the piano, she later chose lessons in church organ, a choice she thinks she made as it is, like piano, a solitary instrument. Eventually, she stopped taking lessons in both instruments as she was not practising. While she loved to play, she found the public side of being a musician confronting; examinations, such a prominent part of music instrumental education for children in Australia, were anathema to her. At primary school she was introduced to the recorder by one of Melbourne's best school recorder teachers, and played in a consort involving the full range of instruments. She recalled that her teachers recognised that she had a special talent for music, and believed that the influence of excellent music teachers was very important for her. At home, she listened to classical music, as well as musical comedy and, later, rock and roll.

When she started working with the children at the centre, she was playing flute and recorder regularly, as well as a small Indian harmonium, the latter deriving from an interest in her own personal faith. Professionally, she was teaching individual children recorder at a primary school in Melbourne with a long tradition in music education.

Lesley's philosophy about music was strong, passionate and clearly articulated. Her views about music were formed by her own experiences as a musician, including her experiences as a child. She explained the nature of music and music-making in this way:

> Music is a language, a form of self-expression. Everyone has a relationship to music of some sort. Of course, it communicates who we are and who we are in relationship to each other and the world around us. It is very empowering, makes connections between people and the world, and to ourselves, first. It is everything, the universe, a whole world, a way of perceiving the world. (Interview, 21 September 2004)

Similarly, her understanding of how children should be engaged in music was filtered through her own experience of music and belief about the nature of music.

She thought that children find music holistically engaging. Her awareness of the potential for music to cause anxiety under some circumstances led to a belief that children should be supported in their musical endeavours, and not be pushed or judged. Children needed to be supported, but then extended. She considered that, in educational settings, there was a possibility for some children to feel excluded: 'There is an exclusivity that I am not comfortable with.' She consequently wanted to be inclusive in her approach: 'The music I do is based on the philosophy that everyone is included and has a voice, a valid voice.' She considered that 'when people, not just children, feel comfortable, without feeling they are being judged, they will contribute their voice'. Furthermore, music, if 'from the heart, has a lovely sound'. She felt she would make mistakes along the way, but that this would not matter because the music would be 'spontaneous and from the heart' (interview, 21 September 2004).

Lesley had taught music to individual children previously, but had never worked with such young children, or groups of children, in a programme where there was an integrated arts programme. Seeking some guidance, early on she attended early childhood conferences that she considered important. 'I drew strongly from my experiences of presentations at, and material and resources drawn from, the annual Early Childhood Conference of Performing Arts (ECCPA) presented by the Victorian Orff Schulwerk Association (VOSA)' (personal communication, 20 June 2014).

This conference was regularly attended by one of the researchers, and two other musicians also were familiar with VOSA. This influence runs through the following chapters, as well as the work of Kodaly.

The research

When the two researchers who were involved in the project initially were asked to document the music programme at the centre, Lesley was already working with each group of children for a weekly hour-long session, in the *boorai* gallery space. The researchers were invited to observe two three-year-old groups during their weekly session. As visiting researchers, we considered carefully how our presence in the sessions might be as unobtrusive as possible, and so chose to take on the role of participant observers (Kawulich, 2005). Working as a pair, one researcher would sit quietly on the floor taking observation notes and photographs while the other joined in the activities as appropriate. For example, one of the researchers, a musician in her own right, could accompany a song on the piano when needed, and both were able to join in singing and in games and activities. While the children were accustomed to being observed by visitors in their sessions, Lesley was new to this process and negotiated her own level of comfort; the researchers were aware of this circumstance, and often talked with Lesley informally about the project and the processes, as well as sharing their experiences and perceptions of the sessions.

As noted, data was collected in a range of ways: observation notes, still photographs and videos (taken at times by a staff member of the centre as part of their own research); an interview with the musician and the musician's plans for each session, along with the reports of the sessions, were both displayed in the passageway for the centre's community to peruse. As the first to conduct formal music sessions, Lesley had to devise her own way of planning and communicating these plans. Hour sessions for young children can be problematic, but there was never a sense in these sessions that children were not involved; levels and types of involvement differed, but the time seemed to pass quickly. Lesley's thoughtful planning was a major contributor to this.

Session plans

Specialist teachers were required to display weekly plans and session reports, or reflections, in the passageway. For guidance, they were given a copy of the centre objectives for music. This document was divided into units and the director provided a copy (Director, interview, 29 May 2014). The overall objective was to encourage 'creating' and the general objective was 'for each child to have the opportunity to hear and explore a variety of musical experiences'. The document was then divided into three units:

- Unit 1 was an exploration of musical experiences; the objectives for this unit included exploring sounds, instruments, body percussion, use of voice and emotional response to music.
- Unit 2 was called 'making'; this involved becoming aware of musical concepts like pitch, tempo, duration, timbre, beat, rhythm and dynamics.
- Unit 3 was presenting; the emphasis here was to share music-making with others.

The specialists were also informed of current centre projects and programme focus so this could be incorporated into the planned experiences if possible. In this way, the children could explore issues, concepts and ideas from a range of arts perspectives, and there was a connectedness across the various modes of exploration being used in the arts programme.

The session plans Lesley displayed in the passage indicated her intentions to embed her sessions in the wider context of the programme interests being pursued, enriching the children's experience of their environment, both local and wider, through musical activities. Lesley's stated session objectives often started with a generic objective 'for the children to engage with enjoyment, confidence and increasing ability in a range of musical activities'. Her plans were then set out in vertical rows with an objective presented for a number of designated learning areas. These were:

- Developing the language of music
- Skills, techniques and materials

- Responding to music
- Enquiry-based learning
- Music and other key learning areas.

Lesley stated that she was greatly influenced by the Orff approach and had attended some conferences. Her approach to planning had the breadth and enthusiasm that VOSA brought to the conferences presented for early childhood teachers and musicians. Richard Gill on VOSA's website, says:

> In a child's life it is often the music teacher who will be remembered above all others once the child has left school. Music teachers have the potential to turn the ordinary into the extraordinary, sparking imaginations at every turn. You never know when this happens with a child, which makes every lesson special, no matter how hard it may seem at the time. Music teachers are the salt of the earth. (VOSA, 2014)

At the ECCPA conferences, VOSA promoted musical exploration and experience in a variety of modes, including an emphasis on the benefits of music and the arts as part of life's journey, on music as part of a holistic approach to education and valuing the integration of music concepts into daily events.

Lesley's plans reflected this broad approach. A weekly plan for the five groups of children in June 2005 is an example. In the first category of 'developing the language of music', she planned for the children to learn a tune by 'following the direction of hand gestures' and for the children to experience creating different 'words' and 'lyrics' to songs. In the skills and techniques section, she planned for the use of finger cymbals to accompany a song, listening to a poem and singing with a recorded song. In the response section, she introduced an animal puppet and pursued the manipulation of the puppet to illustrate enquiry-based learning as the children played with the puppet and discussed how this creature, a possum, would move, live and react to night and day. Her final statement for this week, under the category of key learning areas, was:

> Music evolves the holistic development of the child – not only his/her musical ability but also across many parameters of social, physical, intellectual and affective development. Music also engenders feelings of connectedness, appreciation and beauty, and fosters a sense of meaningfulness. (Lesley, weekly music plan, 2 June 2005)

Lesley's written report on the music sessions of that week, titled 'Music with Lesley', had less philosophy, but expanded on the story by listing exactly what had been achieved in terms of use of the variety of repertoire planned. The children sang about possums and bell birds and continued to explore the theme of the river. They learned a new bell bird song, sang the bell bird chorus they were familiar with, played the finger cymbals and sang to a CD. Following this, they played a guessing game (the answer was a possum) and sang three possum songs with the hand puppet. These songs were familiar ones; the children changed the words to fit the possum's activities.

Lesley's plans were unique, reflecting her own beliefs about music, children and life; she was able to successfully frame her work in the ELC as there was a resonance between her own ideas and the aims and objectives of the arts programme at the centre. She discovered specific guidance for her work with young children through VOSA, which philosophically shared her holistic view of music in the life of a child. She drew her repertoire from a variety of places, using stories, songs, games, movement, words and silence to advance her craft.

Use of repertoire

Lesley adopted material from many sources because it suited the purpose and, therefore, there was a great variety of musical styles and activities collected to present to the children. Lesley kept these in a spiral-bound book with a plastic cover; her ideas were written, or photocopied, and kept in plastic sleeves within the book. This book was usually placed on the floor, in front of the scene that Lesley would set up each week. The book and the scene were essential parts of Lesley's repertoire. The use of the scene-setting is described below in the little green frog observation (see Figure 3.2). The children's awareness of the book and its contents are included in the learning story about the child using her pointing index finger to control her pitch in Chapter 8.

Observing Lesley's sessions, there was a sequence that was followed for each session. On arrival in the gallery, children would remove their shoes and sit in a circle while examining the scene on the floor in front of them. Lesley would then sing the 'Hello' song. This became a ritual song across all groups. In the folder of music there is a photocopy of this song (source unknown). It is described as 'Tonality: Aeolian' and 'Meter: Duple' and Lesley has written 'descending 4th'. There are suggestions of how this song can be used at the bottom of the page, one being to let each child sing their name in the penultimate line. Lesley, realising this would turn into a somewhat repetitive experience, has written in 'Hello children'; in the last line they can sing 'Hello Lesley' back. The song also has a riff in the middle that goes 'Ta da dum Ta da dum Ta da da da dum'. When listening to the children singing 'Hello', we noticed that Lesley had turned this riff into 'Pat-a-pon, pat-a-pon ...' which was an enjoyable sequence to sing. The 'Hello' song would sometimes be played by Lesley on the recorder before the singing started. All the material used by Lesley reflected this careful planning, signs of research and her own adaptations of much of the material she used. An example of such adaptations can be found in observation three, presented below, where Lesley adapted the traditional song 'Cuckoo, Where Are You?' to play a musical game about Australian bell birds.

As commented on in the session plan described above, Lesley used a variety of activities to explore music with the children. The children became engaged in the songs because they were linked to stories and themes being discussed, they were a form of play – as familiar songs were chosen and then the words rewritten to illustrate the interest of the moment. Examples of this are to be seen in the lesson plan discussed above, when the children had guessed that the visiting puppet was a possum. The children discussed aspects of possum lore, such as that it has a bushy tail, feeds at night and likes to climb. This knowledge was sung to known songs like 'Go In and Out the Windows', with the possums going in and out the tree hides; 'Hop Old Squirrel', with the possums climbing, eating, hiding and scratching; the final possum song for this session was 'Here Sits a Possum' (music with Lesley, 2 June 2006).

The variety of music Lesley introduced was immense; at the same time, there was a commitment to skill development. While the children were substituting lyrics in songs, Lesley had also recorded that they should begin to pitch to the *solfa* when singing their names. Lesley believed in helping children to sing in tune (e.g., lesson plan, 2 June 2005) and this was part of the holistic approach she had to music. An article in her book of music activities (Carlton, 2006) contained advice about how children could feel at one with the music while singing. 'Sing a greeting song! Sing for a birthday! Sing a goodbye song! ... Sing for the joy of singing! ... please sing with your children in their singing range, and model the pleasure felt when everyone sings together' (n.p.). The advice to follow the children was something that Lesley was philosophically attuned to and her acute ear made this task one that she addressed using thoughtful methods, such as gesture; the children did not seem to notice they were being conducted.

The format of the music sessions followed a pattern in that the children were always introduced to an idea at the beginning, introductory listening and singing would occur with the greeting and then a mix of activities would follow – some linked to the introduction and others more like musical play. There were instruments to be explored and the qualities they contained would be examined as children tried to express the sun, the wind, the river, rain or thunder. Movement games, body percussion, walking to recorded music and singing to recorded music were all part of the repertoire. Children's picture story books and poetry were read, stories told and posters investigated for their meanings – all within a frame of 'developing the language of music'. Perhaps most striking of all was how still the children would sit when music from one of the recorders was played. The single notes seemed to transfix the children; we observed this on many occasions.

To further develop our discussion of Lesley's planning and use of repertoire, the following stories, drawn from the data collected from the music sessions, illustrate the way Lesley worked with the children.

Three observations

Story one: the thunderstorm

Context

The following story is part of an hour-long session in August 2003, drawing particularly on observation notes, photos, Lesley's session plan and report, and the children's drawings at the end of the session.

The children enter the room quietly in pairs, taking their shoes off before, of their own accord, going to sit cross-legged in a circle in the centre of the room. They are immediately interested in seeing what Lesley has set up for them in the display on the floor in the centre of the circle, talk among themselves about what they can see and point objects out to each other. Some get onto hands and knees to get a better view, but nobody touches the display. In this session, the display includes pictures of clouds of various kinds on a blue fabric background, and a selection of percussion instruments are set out in a regular pattern around the edge of the display. There is a rain-maker, some guiros, some wooden tone blocks, a tambour and some colourful egg-shaped shakers.

Once the discussion about the scene in the centre of the circle dies away, Lesley picks up her treble recorder and, without comment, starts to play the melody of the 'Hello' song used at the start of every session. The children watch and listen intently as Lesley adds some melodic variations to the tune they know well before inviting them to sing the song with her; they then sing quietly and tunefully. The 'Hello' song is followed by spoken verse, also used each session:

> Be kind to one another *(arms held out to the side)*
> and every living thing *(arms folded over the chest)*
> the fishes in the water *(hands together indicating the swimming action of fish)*
> the birds upon the wing *(hands imitating bird flight)*

The children say the verse together and perform the hand gestures they use each week to emphasise the meaning of the words.

The children sing one of their favourite songs, 'The Earth is our Mother', and other songs with which they are already familiar. Lesley introduces them to a short poem 'Rain is Falling Down', and introduces a discussion about different kinds of rain and what kinds of sounds rain makes. To introduce the possibility that the percussion instruments on display might be able to make sounds representing rain, Lesley passes the rain-maker around the circle for each child to experience the feeling of the instrument as the beads inside fall gently and slowly through the instrument and the particular sound it makes. Lesley recites the rain poem again, and experimented herself with sounds on the piano to suggest the 'plip' and 'plop' sounds, while the children 'fall down like the rain'. She then sings the song 'Rain is Falling Down' and the children join in with the singing. She divides the children into two groups. One group is given tone blocks and asked to make sounds to indicate 'rain is falling down'. The other children in the second group are invited to make sounds with the shakers to illustrate the sound of 'pitter patter'. Lesley introduces a new song about thunderstorms, singing the song through for the children in an expressive way that helps to illustrate the minor key and dramatic sense of the words. The first line links to the pictures of clouds in the day's scene in the middle of the circle: 'Watch the clouds turn black'. The next lines, 'thunder rolls, lightning bolts' interest the children, and causes one girl to spontaneously tell a complete narrative about a dream her sister had experienced. The children join in, singing the song with Lesley. Silk and muslin scarves are handed out, and Lesley then sings a song to the children about mist, while everybody moves around the room and uses their scarves and bodies to represent mist in their own expressive ways.

The session ends with the 'Goodbye' song, another song used every week to end the session. Before leaving the room the children are invited to draw 'what they enjoyed most in music today'. They spread out on the floor and, using pencils and sheets of paper clipped to boards, draw their response. The teachers and the authors talk to the children as they draw and write their story on the drawings for them. This is part of the data collection process developed by the centre in their ongoing research, and the children were accustomed to the process (Bond and Deans, 1997).

Observation

Part of this story involves an observation of one particular child's experience of this session. The observation notes follow his response to the songs and some of the activities.

> M is a boy and is one of the smaller children in the group. He sits in the circle directly across from the musician leading the group. He is quiet for the orientation. He tips the rain-maker with a serious expression on his face. When the poem 'Rain is Falling' is recited he watches, yawns, watches again and starts to make small rhythmic movements with his hands. On the repeat, he joins in on the word 'sea'. When 'plip, plop' is played on the piano M starts playing one of the wood blocks. He uses two different strokes to differentiate between the 'plip' and the 'plop'. He uses a downward stroke followed by a direct beat or stroke. When this exercise finishes he sits feeling the wood block with his hands. After this exploration, M sucks his thumb and holds his hair. When the song 'Rain is Falling Down' is introduced M is in the group asked to play the falling down part, using a downward stroke. M plays with a direct stroke the first time around and then misses the repetition and joins in for the 'pitter patter'. When the thunderstorm song is sung, M bangs on the wood block at the word 'black'. While the children are discussing thunder he sucks his thumb and holds his head. He looks at the wood block and puts his head down. The song starts again. M looks up quickly and picks up his beater and starts to play the wood block. He joins in on the work 'black' as it is sung at the end of the first line of the song.
>
> When the mist song is sung M takes a scarf and waves it around in the air. He then notices some children have their scarves in front of their faces. He puts his scarf in front of his face and then lowers it and says, 'The sun is out'. His drawing at the end of the session is of the wood block, with the sounds falling out of it.

FIGURE 3.1 M's drawing of the sound falling

Interpretive comments and general discussion

Reflection on the nature of this story reveals aspects of the session that our observations show were characteristic of Lesley's approach to working with the children. Notably, Lesley carefully created a special space for the children to experience music. The nature of the *boorai* art gallery provided a background to this creative process. The room is the size of a classroom, well lit, with a high ceiling, white walls and a plain, carpeted floor. Children's art work is displayed on the walls, framed professionally and displayed with the kind of respect given to adult art works in an adult gallery. The paintings often remained on display for some time, as this is also used for special exhibitions. There is a small, white, upright piano and good-quality classroom music instruments such as African drums and xylophones, all in excellent condition, which are displayed on cupboards. The overall impression of the space is of an uncluttered, light and peaceful place, with a spare aesthetic. This space contrasted with the classroom and outdoor spaces in which the children spent their day. Classrooms at this centre were also used carefully to create interesting and particular spaces for the children, reflecting the interests and activities of the group, respecting the children's work and provoking exploration. These were usually 'busy' and changing spaces, which the children were involved actively in designing as a work in progress. Each week the children would move from this kind of busy classroom space, along the centre's passage, with its public function and design, to the special and quite different arts space created in the *boorai* gallery. This differentiation was emphasised as the children removed their shoes at the door and came to sit quietly in a circle in the middle of the room. The director, influenced partially by the Reggio Emilia example, had designed the overall space to be neutral: 'The space and the objects it contains can have different chromatic characteristics. While it is better for the colour of the overall environment to be predominantly delicate and unobtrusive, the object-landscape can be more colourful' (Ceppi and Zini, 1998, p. 66). This was the space in which Lesley was able to create her own particular musical aesthetic for the children.

Lesley worked within this room quite deliberately to create her own music space. The scene set up for the children each week in the centre of the circle acted as an immediate focus, capturing the children's attention as they looked for visual clues to the content of the day's session, and references to previous sessions. The displays were uncluttered, designed simply to stimulate thought, imagination and speculation. In the example presented here (Figure 3.2), the children easily recognised that the watercolour pictures from story books on a blue fabric background was a reference to the sky, to kinds of clouds and, perhaps, to weather. Lesley refrained from directing conversation about the display, letting the children discuss among themselves what they saw. The inclusion of musical instruments, set out neatly in categories and all chosen from those with which the children were familiar, might stimulate ideas about the nature of the music-making in store during the session. This carefully constructed aspect of the space was a thread running through sessions from week to week, forming an activity that was recognised by the children as a part of the music session that they routinely looked forward to.

As described above, the same greeting song was used every week; it seemed to act as a framing activity, setting the session apart from the rest of the day, and as a means of re-establishing the ongoing relationship between the musician and the children, as well as reinforcing the sense that the children had come to a separate and special space. With her use of space, Lesley created a culture of thoughtfulness for the children. Her introduction of the greeting song, without announcement, playing the melody musically and quietly on a treble recorder with small melodic variations departing slightly from the well-known melody, was also part of this framing, routine activity, and the children's intent attention indicated their engagement in the aesthetics of this strategy. The poem that followed similarly formed part of the introduction, reminding the children that they were in a special 'music' place. The session finished with a 'Goodbye' song, also used each week, similarly providing a framing function for the session, and adding to the sense that this was a special space in their day.

This description of this session also showed Lesley playing with the idea of the 'constants', those threads that tie one session to the next, providing a sense of continuity for the children. This idea is further developed by the third musician's deliberate use of the relationship between the familiar and the unfamiliar to develop competence in engaging with musical concepts (Chapter 5). The 'constants' of the session – ritual songs and verse, and the use of the scene in the circle – were not overt, but were rather an aspect of the session that the children tended to perceive for themselves, and to enjoy. In this case, the visual display in the centre of the circle included a stylised representation of the local river, a cue well understood by the children from previous sessions, as well as some new material. This was a child-directed activity that indicated that the children were accustomed to looking for visual reminders and cues in this way each week.

The children's attention to Lesley's improvisation around the 'Hello' song melody suggested that this was a regular aspect of the orientation to the session that the children looked forward to. Singing the 'Hello' song and saying the verse together, along with the 'Goodbye' song, similarly provided continuity for the children, as well as adding to the sense that the physical musical space and the musical time are framed by the special and the familiar. Here, Lesley's use of cues was subtle; the process of improvisation of shared melody could be considered an unusual strategy to gain a sense of involvement from such young children. Such an action reflected Lesley's stated philosophy that children have a holistic relationship to music, and have the capacity to engage with languages like music at a higher level, reminiscent of the theories of Vygotsky that learning can lead development (Vygotsky, 1978).

This session plan indicated that Lesley wanted to develop the children's ability to experience the expressive aspects of music as well as developing specific musical skills needed to understand and participate actively in music. As listed above, her plans each week included investigating the components: the language of music, skills techniques and materials, responding to music, enquiry-based learning and connections between music and other key learning areas. Within this framework, she planned for a variety of activities designed to engage young children for an hour-long session, and to share a very personal view of what music is like and how children might be active musicians in their own right.

The session described above included the introduction of vocal *ostinato* (repeated patterns or phrases), an activity not included in the above story. The need for children to have a developed, internalised 'inner beat' for this activity to work means that this is an activity the literature suggests is unlikely to be successful with young children (Bayless and Ramsay, 1991). Nevertheless, the children were encouraged to use vocal phrases as *ostinati* to accompany 'Rain is Falling Down' and 'Doctor Foster', both songs they knew well, and while the results were rhythmically a little awry, the experience of 'accompanying' was real, and the children were encouraged in their music-making. The children were, however, well able to demonstrate their understanding of fast and slow tempo, as distinct from loud and soft dynamics, through a range of activities throughout the session – for example, by exploring soft and loud through body percussion, later transferred to suitable percussion instruments. These explorations were sometimes clearly directed, as in the *ostinato* patterns for the songs, but sometimes only directed by the provision of suitable instruments and a discussion with the children about the different sound possibilities they might find. M's depiction of the music falling from his wood block in his drawing at the end of the session suggested that this opportunity for exploration of sound possibilities captured his imagination in a way perhaps not possible in the more directed, skills-based activities.

The session included many songs, some well known and some new to the children. At times, Lesley was happy to sing a song for the children to listen to, or, perhaps, to play the melody of a well-known song on her treble recorder, in the same way as they might listen to a story or a poem. The children's singing was quiet and in tune, a far cry from the usual enthusiastic roar more common for a group of three-year-old children. The literature suggests that, although these children would be typically enthusiastic about singing a quite large repertoire of songs, would enjoy singing both on their own and in a group, be likely to invent their own songs (perhaps using snippets of known material) and are capable of imitating short songs, their pitch accuracy is not likely to be well developed until about five years (Pound and Harrison, 2003; Young, 2004). While it may be that children find it more challenging to sing in tune because of immature vocal cord development, our observations of the children's singing in Lesley's sessions suggest that their consistent experience of a single, light and often unaccompanied voice, singing their songs, directly for them, musically and with respect, led to the children naturally imitating the tone and pitch of Lesley's vocal model. She tried to make the key she chose for a song accessible to the children by listening to their attempts and changing the key if necessary. At times, Lesley used her hand to indicate change in pitch within a song, a kind of simplified and generalised version of the more formal hand signs used in methods such as Kodaly. Some children noticed this strategy and imitated the movements, but Lesley chose not to comment on it at all, rather letting her hand movements support pitch-change for those children who responded. In Chapter 8, we unpack an example of a child in one of Lesley's sessions spontaneously using a pointing finger to follow her own pitch changes within a song. The quality of the singing in the sessions was a source of immediate, sensitive music, directly accessible to the children.

Songs came from the traditional song repertoire: 'Doctor Foster', 'Rain is Falling Down', 'The Earth is Our Mother'; some were developed more recently, such as 'Hello', 'It's Time To Sing Goodbye Now', 'The Thunderstorm' and 'It Rained a Mist'. Some were repeated regularly, as a means of emphasising the sense of the special music time and space; 'The Earth is Our Mother' was so popular across the ELC that it was frequently sung at the centre assemblies. In the sessions discussed here, including the one below, many songs were chosen deliberately to support the environmental focus throughout the centre.

Story two: the little green frog

Context

During this session, Lesley invited the children to explore the world of frogs, drawing on the children's familiarity with the world of the river in their local environment. They stepped around the room, pretending to walk to the river together,
along their usual path, and tried out different ways to walk, exploring the musical
concepts of dynamics and duration as they sang 'We're all off to the river along the
Yarra track', stepping out the beat of the song in 'seven league boots' and in 'fairy
slippers'. The river environment is also represented imaginatively in a picture displayed for the children in the centre of their circle. The song was adapted from
Kleiner's (2000) adaptation of 'Off to the River'. This was a resource Lesley came
across at the ECCPA conference.

Observation

This observation was recorded through photographs and field notes compiled after
the event. Figure 3.2 is a photograph of the scene that introduced the children to
the activity of the little green frog.

As frogs hopping into the water, the children experienced the feeling of contrac-
tion and of expansion as the ripples in the water flowed out (from musician's report

FIGURE 3.2 The scene for the 'Little Green Frog' song

of the session, 26 August 2005). They sang frog songs that expressed a range of moods, including the sombre mood suggested by a song in a minor key.

This is the story of the last activity in the hour, and draws particularly on observation notes and photographs. The activity reflects Lesley's intention to try a carefully constructed and fairly directed activity. The children were invited to help tell the story of the 'Little Green Frog' through song and the playing of selected instruments with which they were already familiar. This song tells of the adventure of a 'little green frog [that] lived under a log, near a pond, by the fence, in the garden' (Matterson, 1991, pp. 249–51), using the well-loved repetitive structure that allows children to enjoy the piling up of text and melody. Lesley drew the children's attention to the instruments she had carefully set out for them as part of the day's display, and wondered, aloud, on the nature of the different instruments and on the sounds they might make. Since the instruments were chosen from those well known to the children, Lesley was able to ask them to remember the instrumental sounds, and to imagine how those sounds might be able to illustrate the story-line of the song. There were tone blocks and guiros to suggest the frog's croak, tambours to suggest the log, finger cymbals for the garden, tambourines to provide a 'splash' and a 'splosh'. The children, through eye gaze, stillness and body language, indicated they were engaged in this quiet time of reflection as they remembered and imagined sounds. Once the instruments had been distributed around the circle, the children listened carefully as they took turns to make the sounds, and talked together about the sounds in the song story. Exploration and discussion resulted in some unconventional ways to play the available instruments. One child carefully and deliberately placed a tone block with guiro-like serrations on the floor in an idiosyncratic choice to produce exactly the slightly 'dampened' sound he wanted for the frog's croak. Another child competently grasped the heavy rose-wood rhythm sticks to produce the clear, bright sound she wanted to mark the regular rhythm of the pickets in the fence in the song, while another ran a beater around the inside of a small, circular xylophone-like instrument for the same purpose (see Figure 3.3).

Interpretive comment and general discussion

Lesley directed this activity carefully, first through the choice of instruments provided for the children to explore for specific purposes in the song story and then through her direction of the children's attention to the sounds of specific instruments. This is an unusually directed approach for young children, but the song story's framework provided a carefully constructed space in which to experiment with the instruments and their sounds, and within which to make musical choices. It is likely that the children were used to working this way. Inserting the instrumental sounds into the appropriate section of the song while also singing is clearly a complex task for young children. Some seemed to focus mostly on managing their instrument, often quite large and heavy in young hands, to produce the sound in their imagination and relied on Lesley's direction to know where to

FIGURE 3.3 The tone block guiro

place the sound in the song. Others seemed to be listening carefully to the pattern of the song, and were not so focused on their sounds. Few managed to sing as well as play, leaving Lesley, the home-room teacher and the visiting researchers to do most of the singing. Possibly a 'trained' teacher would be unlikely to attempt such a complex task, and be daunted by the logistics involved in setting the activity up. All the same, in this case, clearly individual children were engaged by different aspects of the activity. Lesley refrained from drawing attention to any musical inaccuracies in what was otherwise a directed and structured activity, but offered encouragement.

Story three: bell birds

Context

The third story describes a short segment of a session that also focused on the environment. Lesley frequently took account of the centre's garden setting and of the children's relationship with and innate attraction to the nearby river and the bush park along its banks. Although the centre is close to the city, the proximity of bush-land meant that the children were familiar with some native birds, including the bell miner that frequents open bushland. This bird is usually called a bell bird, in refer-ence to its clear, bright, single bell-like call. The bird's plumage ensures that it is well camouflaged, and the children all agree that, although everyone can hear a bell bird, nobody ever sees one.

Observation

During the session, Lesley stops what she is doing, and listens intently, with her head on one side. She asks if anyone can hear the bell bird, and the children also listen intently. She crosses to the window to open it so that everyone could hear. The children seem to hear an imaginary bell bird in the distance and some spon-taneously imitate the single bell-like call. Opening the window brings the outside into the room, and the window remains open during the following song game. One child is invited to hide under a large green gauze scarf (because you can always hear bell birds, but never see them). The 'bell bird' is given a pair of finger cymbals and, after the class sings 'Bell bird, where are you? Bell bird, where are you?' on a falling minor third, the hidden child imitates the sound of the bell bird, using the cymbals. The rest of children eagerly 'discover' where the bell bird is hiding, peering under the scarf and pointing out the hiding spot to each other and Lesley.

Interpretive comment and general discussion

This activity had been carefully constructed to engage the children's interest in the familiar, in a playful way that encouraged memories of past experiences and imagined possibilities. The children were happy to invest the bell bird with a kind of magical mystery, tapping into the characteristic elusiveness the bell bird holds for everyone. Their spontaneous imitation of the bird's call early in the activity indicated an existing interest in the bird, and their immediate engage-ment with the pretence. Their drawings at the end of the session bore out their enjoyment of the notion of 'being' a bell bird and making the bell bird's sound, both with their voices and with an instrument. As usual, the children were invited to draw whatever they liked from the hour-long session and staff collected their drawings to find what narrative was dominant in their memories from the ses-sion. The bell bird game elicited many drawings – for example, 'I drawed about music today and then I drawed a bell bird.' Another child explained 'That's a path and that's where you go,' possibly recalling paths by the river where you can hear bell birds. One child drew a tambourine, 'The tambourine (boom, boom, boom)'. The teacher noted, 'The tambourine was not used today, but W says that he likes it.'

"... I drawed about :- music today and Oscar
then I drawed a bell-bird." - 18·5·15

FIGURE 3.4 Bell bird

Concluding discussion

In this chapter we have introduced Lesley, the first of the three specialist musicians who worked in this arts programme. We have discussed Lesley's musical background and identified some of the major influences on her beliefs and methods when working with young children. Her research for materials was eclectic, which we have illustrated by introducing her style of lesson planning; we have also discussed her use of repertoire. To indicate the children's involvement in the music sessions three observations/stories were chosen as they can be said to be representative of the experience the children had in sessions with Lesley. The first has been more intensively commented upon to give context to Lesley's sessions.

Like all the other arts specialists, Lesley was not a trained teacher and, consequently, was free to be governed in her work by her own well-articulated philosophy about music, music-making and the place of music in the lives of children, unmediated, to an extent, by the expectations that come with teacher training. In a sense, as was the nature of the *atelierista* in the Reggio Emilia approach, this allowed her to share her own views and skills about music – as an adult, practising musician – with the children in her own very particular way, according to what she believed music experiences should offer children.

A thread that runs strongly through each session is the sense that music and music-making is treated with respect, as something unique. The sense of a special space, both physical and musical, already provided by the nature of the *boorai* gallery, which Lesley chose to elaborate, means that the children's experience of music had a certain quiet, calm aesthetic that reflected Lesley's view that music-making should not be a cause of anxiety for children. She was willing to provide challenges, such as the musical techniques and skills involved in the more structured part of the frog song, and often the children rose to the occasion with unexpected competence; she was not inclined to draw attention to any technical shortcomings. Indeed, her ability to follow the children in an atmosphere where expectations didn't dominate meant that children often produced musical results that were quite striking. Her acceptance of a range of responses in the context of challenges seemed to bear out her view that children should be extended, but in a culture of support and encouragement.

As was to be expected, while Lesley had a strong view of the nature of music and music-making, from her own perspective as an adult, practising musician, she necessarily needed to feel her way with her work with the children. The range of approaches, from quite structured to more playful, indicated that, as she said, she knew she would perhaps makes mistakes along the way (interview, 21 July 2005). To undertake this level of exploration with other adults, including the children's teachers and the two researchers – all trained teachers – in the room, was surely a challenging task. She had hoped that stumbles would not matter if the children were spontaneous in their music-making and expression, and our observations suggest that this was the case.

Lesley's session plans were idiosyncratic. Each session included both technical musical skills and knowledge, such as the ability to understand the nature of dynamics and the opportunity to play with and respond to that concept, or the opportunity to show the beat or pulse of a song though body percussion and percussion instruments. Lesley was also able to use tonality to help explore expressive possibilities, such as in the minor key for the song about a thunderstorm. As well, her capacity to hear where the children's voices sat allowed her to adjust the pitch of a song to suit them.

Each session supported the centre's programme interests, particularly the environment (which suited Lesley's own preferences for content), but the intention to allow the children to engage with music holistically, as an expressive art form, seemed to be predominant. A strong interest in the nature of music as a language, as a means of self-expression, ran through her work. The story of M's response to the storm song, in the first observation above, provided insight into the ways individual children were able to engage with even quite structured activities in a very individual way, finding a way to express what Lesley referred to as their own 'voice'. The bell bird story, which seemed to develop according to its own momentum once Lesley had started the story by opening the window and listening to the outside world, was an example of a far less structured approach, in which the children, as a group, were able to find a voice. Indeed, the children's drawings at the end of each session showed that the ways in which children chose to engage in any one session were widely varied, and reflected individual perspectives and voices. These sessions go beyond the idea of self-expression as children engage with musical experiences founded on the musician's own philosophy and search for meaning and connections and artistry.

As the first musician to undertake the task of presenting formal music sessions in the ELC programme, Lesley was treading on ground that had not been explored. The timetable was dictated by the centre timetable and the hour-long session in a designated place away from daily activities was also set. That Lesley sought support in ideas of working with young children from VOSA was coincidence, as such an approach suited her own personal inclinations, provided her with a variety of resources and the confidence to seek out her own, and found a fit with the centre's own objectives about the importance of art and the notion of artistry (Director, interview, 29 May 2014).

4

SINGING

A way of life

Introduction

The musician, Leah, in this story had a background in community music which spread beyond the children to the educators in the centre. Leah played guitar and drums, among other instruments, and had spent time in Europe, Egypt and South America. Leah's background was diverse: she was born in Montreal and has a Hungarian and Egyptian heritage. Consequently, she had experienced varied styles of music and languages across a number of contexts. Her music teaching involved a wide range of songs, and a richness of ideas. While the music of the first musician, Lesley, was also rich, it tended to be drawn from music prepared specifically for children. Both these musicians had an interest in expressing ideas about the environment, social justice and peace through their music. As well as managing the children's music sessions, Leah was responsible for conducting the staff singing group that led to a shared repertoire for the children and the staff, companion singing and singing in harmony, culminating in a performance for parents and siblings.

This chapter discusses Leah's work at the ELC. Leah described her musical background as one grounded in piano and music theory; she was self-taught on drums and guitar. Playing piano had been a big part of her early life and she had been involved in choirs and singing groups. Her home life was musical: 'Mum could turn anything into a song. I also have a dance background.' Leah was involved in community singing and felt 'there is a feeling of health and well-being that comes through singing' (interview, 6 June 2008). She had completed a Steiner diploma of education and her musical interests were culturally eclectic. As a specialist in the arts programme, she enjoyed the strong connections she was able to develop with the children and regretted there was not more time to also work with parents and the other arts specialists. The activities Leah was involved in included the development of the staff singing group, which was established to support the idea of singing as a community activity, writing what turned out to be a signature tune for the Antarctica project (Chapters 2 and 8) and preparing weekly plans to share with staff and parents. These plans were displayed on the notice board in the corridor.

As a specialist in the programme, Leah delivered weekly music sessions to the different groups of children, played a role in the children's assemblies and participated in themes adopted as part of the *Let're Verde* programme the centre joined with each year. In this chapter we discuss relationships (both physical and social) within the music programme, the value of community singing and how a belief in group singing across the ELC community influenced musical activities. The involvement of children and adults increased opportunities for relational complexities.

The role of the music specialist in the centre projects has been mentioned in each chapter and Leah took on a different role when she returned to the centre for a while when Kylie (Chapter 5) was delivering the formal music sessions. When Leah returned to the centre, she participated in an enterprise that involved visiting and singing with the children in their rooms. This was at the instigation of the director, who was interested in expanding the music programme beyond the gallery. She hoped for a shared repertoire across the rooms and each room educator would have the chance to work with Leah and gain skills in a one-to-one partnership. Leah was enthusiastic about this initiative as it found a resonance with her own ideas about singing and the formation of communities.

The data for this chapter included interview material, three interviews with Leah, one interview each with the staff who participated in the singing group, music plans, formal reflections and photographs of the children during music sessions.

Relationships

The idea of discussing relationships as both physical and social refers to the physical space the music programme occupied and how this space helped to define the music activities. The other aspect of relationships that existed within the centre was the complexity of relationships between the specialists and generalist teachers, the specialists themselves, the children relating to adults who played different roles in their daily lives, children and children, and the role of parents and the director. Leah was thoughtful about the relationships that existed within the centre and the potential of some of those relationships. She explained the role of the specialist programmes, commenting on the specialist role:

> They play a useful role. Can be inspiring for general teachers in their day-to-day practice. An aim of this programme is to bring a strong sense of musicality that the teachers can pick up. I haven't worked in the rooms, but I think it is valuable if music can be child-directed. The specialist role focuses on specific skills – things like repertoire – and gives children a deep immersion for a while in music that can carry on in their play through the week. (Interview, 6 June 2008)

The emphasis on skill formation could be seen through the session plans of the three musicians. This was also a relational space in that the centre gave Lesley, Leah and Kylie the suggestion of using the strategy of developing templates to communicate their weekly plans. The example template tended to privilege skill development and an exploration of musical concepts. These plans were displayed in the corridor for the other staff and parents.

Apart from the music specialist space that Leah filled while working at the centre in this role as already mentioned, she later took on another role of taking music to the rooms. She returned to the centre when Kylie was the music specialist because she and the director wanted to explore the idea of actively sharing music across the centre rooms. This meant that Leah was working with staff and children in their own space, was sharing rather than delivering and was devising strategies like helpful puppets to assist in storytelling and music-making to help these sessions seem relaxed. She said:

> Storytelling was also a big part of it for me – I would often create a little story to give the song a meaningful context that the children could relate to. If the song had more complex lyrics or ideas, it enabled the song to 'live' in the children's imagination more, and always contributed to easier and quicker learning of the song. One example was what we called 'Peter's Song' (true name 'Da Da Dum', by Paradise Oskar, from the Eurovision Song Contest, 2011), with its strong theme of environmental care and stewardship. The children loved it, and it was amazing how quickly they learned all the lyrics. (Interview, 11 June 2014)

Leah, therefore, had been a musical leader in the centre as a specialist, had participated in the staff singing group as leader and conductor and had worked more collaboratively with staff during the time she visited the rooms. This range of different roles and relationships with the staff and children in the centre was an attempt to bring a 'musical culture' to the centre. This was very important to Leah.

Physical space

> This space! I love it. There is a beautiful presence. The shelves, the instruments on display, the piano. Use of space for movement. When I go to the rooms for music it is very different. (Interview, 17 June 2008)

The music space was the *Boorai* gallery, described in Chapter 2. This space had an aesthetic that was influenced by the Reggio Emilia approach. Aesthetics have citizenship rights in the Reggio Emilia centres (Rinaldi, 2006) and the same concentration on a coherent aesthetic was apparent in the ELC music space. The walls were white to best display the panels of children's work that had been mounted around the room. These were not overwhelming and were hung from a picture rail; there was no impression of crowding. The white piano against one wall stood out and instruments on display on natural wood shelves were Orff-style instruments in natural wood or metal. The carpet was a plain dark blue and the windows had natural wood surrounds and wooden venetian blinds. Leah would bring a basket of brightly coloured flowers, like poinsettia, to add a touch of drama to the room. The basket was always carefully arranged and there was only one kind of flower at any one time. Leah also brought her own drums to add to the displays.

The gallery and the sense of place engendered was a teaching tool in its own right. This was a peaceful, uncluttered large space with natural light and the view from the window contained branches, leaves and flashes of sky. The ceiling was high and the room had been enhanced to support the sound environment. Sense of place is often considered an important part of childhood, often an outdoor space, a place where children experience an emotional bond that can trigger memories and guide aesthetic preferences in adulthood. This room is such a space. The 19th-century building had proportions that were generous and quite beautiful and the present occupants had designed the music space in a way that did not disturb the original lines. The room was at the end of the corridor, away from the children's home-rooms, and the children could be heard talking excitedly, sometimes singing, as they approached the room. As Leah said, she loved the space and found the rooms very different, even though she liked encountering children in their own rooms as a means of taking the music out of its own space to spread it more widely.

Of the three musicians observed in this space, Leah was the one who put a physical reminder of herself in the area each week. The flower basket was the most common, as well as a consistent array of copper pots and coloured scarves. Like Lesley, she would put a display in the middle of the room that was suggestive of the music content to be introduced that day, but the flash of red poinsettias was some-thing that expressed a unique message about her and her relationship to the space which went beyond didactic concerns with the programme. In the music plans, included in this chapter, there are examples of Leah's use of space to represent her own ideas. In lesson five (see below), she introduced a song, 'Light a Candle for Peace', and in a photo taken at the end of the session the children are lying in a circle with a tableau in the centre with a candle. Leah said in her notes for that week:

> We then learned a new song, a very gentle one called 'Light a Candle for Peace'. To get a sense for the mood of the song, we did a meditation lying down listening to some beautiful peaceful music. We remembered a time when we felt happy and peaceful and imagined some situations which might invoke that feeling. We imagined lighting a candle in our hearts that sent beautiful, warm golden light all throughout our bodies. We then brought our 'candles' and our peace back into the circle to learn and sing this new song. A very beautiful way to finish our music class for this week. (10–11 June 2008)

Leah had a strong sense of place and this, in a sense, probably fed into her sense of community and the ways in which people can feel connected to each other. She, therefore, found her sense of place in singing with others and from this convic-tion she developed the initiative that became the staff singing group.

Social space

In an interview (10 June 2008), Leah discussed her thoughts about the relationships across the centre. She enjoyed the physical space of the gallery but would also sometimes help out in the room as a relief general staff member. She used this opportunity to do spontaneous music with the children and this was the origin of the idea of having her visit the rooms with her music and her puppets after she returned to the centre for a short while before moving interstate. By this time, the children were exploring *The Magic Flute* with Kylie (Chapter 5) and the director asked Leah to expand the music activities of the centre by taking her skill into the rooms. An observation of one of these sessions is described in the chapter about the teacher Suzana (Chapter 6).

As a music specialist, Leah had little contact with the parents and thought 'that doesn't seem quite right, not having that connection. Occasionally I meet someone or get some feedback.' There was also little connection with the other artists working in the centre initially: 'We are like ships in the night.' Leah added that it was 'inspiring when I do run into the others. It helps me to understand what learning is going on in the children's worlds' (interview, 17 June 2008). This changed when the staff singing group was established. The director of the centre and Leah seemed to have separately come to the conclusion that a staff initiative might support the children's music. Leah said:

> I brought a song to a staff curriculum day. The staff sang the song and I enjoyed the feeling of community. We have had a couple of sessions after meetings. I'm involved with Community Music Victoria and they promote getting together through singing. (Interview, 17 June 2008)

This was the spirit that Leah brought to her practice: a belief in singing as a socially cohesive activity and one that could break down some of the barriers that existed between the specialist space and the rooms. She thought of singing together as a joint cultural activity and participants would co-construct meanings about music within this context by their actions. Leah also enjoyed the dedicated music space. The value of music as a community activity that could engender well-being among participants was also an area where Leah was an activist and she brought this enthusiasm to the ELC.

Community singing

Leah was involved in community singing and this influenced her music and the work she did with the children and the staff at the ELC. While loving the space she worked in, she also wanted to see connections growing between those at the centre and the different spaces people occupied. One way was to share singing among the adults and the other was to move outside of the physical space of the gallery.

While working as an itinerant teacher across the rooms of the centre for a while, she found a fit with her commitment to music 'as part of life'. She thought that it would have been possible to have more music and less formal music in the centre. She thought for a little while that, after the singing group initiative (discussed below), there was more space for music in the rooms, but then it faded. She felt teachers needed time and 'mental space', and for a short time the mental space was created. Her travels around the rooms were conceived to bring music into familiar spaces daily. It is interesting to note that her sessions with the children in the rooms tended to take the same form as her formal sessions in that a group was conducted with a warm-up, musical point and wind-down exercises. Stories and puppets were used for these sessions; they were less formal, as the children were in their own space and the room teachers were active participants.

Creating a shared music space in the adult community of the centre was initially done by taking 'a song to a staff curriculum day'. The success of this action led to Leah and the director deciding that a staff singing group could be established. The director wanted this activity to be written up as research and, therefore, aims were formulated and a formal ethics application was submitted to the university specifically to observe the singing project. The aims, as formulated, were to examine the role and impact of the specialist programmes within this centre by:

- exploring the role and positioning of the specialist music teacher in an adult initiative (a staff singing group) at the ELC and
- studying the impact of the staff singing group in developing a collaborative relationship among staff in relation to the presence of music in and across the programme.

By making this a research activity, the director hoped to see how this collaborative interest, set up as a formal project, would influence the music in the centre. Leah was more inclined to support a spontaneous structure, but did agree that organising the singing group as formal research initially ensured it got off the ground. She hoped the staff would continue to support such an endeavour themselves after the formal phase, one term and a concert, were concluded. Participation in the group was voluntary and the research was framed to examine the singing exercise as a community of practice (Wenger, 1998), with positioning theory (Barnes, 2004) used to explain the participant's perceptions of the experience. Data was collected by participant observation at the singing practice sessions, filming the concert for children at the end of semester and through interviews during the time the singing sessions were conducted and the following year, when the group was no longer operative.

The early childhood literature abounds with the value of music for young children (Bayless and Ramsay, 1987) and singing is often singled out as an activity that promotes emotional well-being and communicative competence, can be a benevolent didactic tool and lends itself to group participation. The singing group of adults established in this centre came together to share a common repertoire of songs, to share their practice and to create a joint event. The data was collected through participant observation, which meant that one of the researchers attended the singing practices, sang with one of the staff groups, recorded unobtrusively and took some photos. The activity itself constituted a community of practice while the positioning of the staff, in relation to the group, was pursued through observations, two rounds of interviews (pre- and post-performance) and then another round of interviews with the participants to ask if they thought the group had a long-term influence on the centre music programme. Three rounds of interviews over a two-year period were, therefore, conducted to explore the progress of the staff singing group research project.

After the initial singing performance, members of staff were asked about their experiences at the rehearsals. They reported that they found the group enjoyable, though some were a little shy and felt challenged when the music leader started experimenting with part singing. One thought it was a 'weird' thing to do, while most of the staff in the first interviews commented on the feeling of camaraderie they felt. Other words used to describe the relationship that existed during singing practice were collegiality, bonding and connectedness (Nyland and Ferris, 2009). The members of the group all commented positively on the experience and there were two unexpected outcomes. One was the enormous emotional reaction the staff experienced straight after the performance.

The other unexpected outcome was the sense of exclusivity that arose between the volunteers in the singing group and those that had not been able to participate. Most reasons for non-participation were practical ones like travel arrangements that could not be altered. The director was especially sensitive to the potential for some staff to feel excluded. The third round of interviews, conducted with staff two years after the singing group enterprise had taken place, revisited the enterprise. It is unusual to revisit a discrete project after such a length of time, but the interviews resulted from an invitation from the director, who sensed that for some staff the singing group was 'unfinished business'. The experience of singing together had obviously been a powerful one for many of the staff members and, for a period of time, many thought their room practices, in relation to music, were more integrated across the centre. By the time these interviews took place the singing group was a thing of the past and the director commented that, at assembly, there was no shared song that all the staff knew; she said, 'We had no song' (Director, interview, 19 May 2010). She was reflective and talked about the changes she had experienced during the singing project in 2008, what she had hoped for and what she envisaged could happen if there was more inclusive responsibility taken for the music in the centre (Director, interview, 19 May 2010). The staff singers thought they had been temporarily empowered, most would do it again and there was a sense that some benefits were still felt in the centre.

As for the singing group itself, the repertoire had consisted of known songs from the rooms, like the 'Diamond Dust' song that had been sung in conjunction with the Antarctic project and other songs, largely introduced by Leah. One evening, an impromptu concert took place as staff members sang and invited others to join in their favourite songs. The sculptor sang 'All the Pretty Little Horses', which made others cry on hearing the verse about the baby in the meadow. Many were not aware that this lullaby has a darker side. The feelings elicited by this song were an indication of how emotionally close this group was prepared to become during their rehearsals and also a reminder of some of the complex adult themes found in songs supposedly developed for very young children in the guise of lullabies and nursery rhymes. Leah described how the repertoire developed:

> I developed a singing programme for the duration of the course, and initially did invite people to contribute songs, though I remember no-one felt comfortable to until further down the track. During the last few weeks, some people did get up the courage to share their songs, I particularly remember Natalie's song was a big hit and did become part of our repertoire, but I can't quite remember the name of it. It was quite significant for her to feel confident to share and teach the song to the group. The impromptu jam/sharing session did take place too and was great fun. (Interview, 9 June 2014)

Leah introduced a traditional American song, 'This Body Lie Down', to be used as a warm-up; then, when it became a familiar song, she moved it onto another level by using the familiar to introduce harmony singing. This strategy of using familiar material to introduce more complex musical play is a method Leah also used with the children (see comments about '*Ume-lay-la*' below). African songs were introduced; the Italian '*Bongiorno Mio Caro*' and traditional English tunes were used for companion singing. These songs were 'Rose, Rose, Rose Red', 'Hey, Ho Nobody at Home' and 'Ah Poor Bird'. These songs were familiar to most of the singers and there was some discussion regarding how, or why, they knew these traditional songs. A favourite song was the Israeli entry into the Eurovision Song Contest in 2002, 'Light a Candle'. All Leah's repertoire suggested that musical diversity was an enduring interest.

The format of the singing group practices followed the format used in the children's sessions. The children's sessions were framed by the template the centre used for music and each musician was given the template, and a copy of a music curriculum devised by the director, to devise their own way of adapting the form to suit their own approach within a suggested paradigm. The sessions took the format of a warm-up session, an introductory song, followed by various songs from the repertoire. Pieces of songs were rehearsed and then put back into the context of the whole song. Instructions like 'throw out the sound' and 'feel the consonants' were given, these latter in relation to the singing of 'Diamond Dust'. Instruments were used – mainly guitar, drum and body percussion. Hands and feet were used for rhythm and beat patterns. These were similar to the children's experiences. For this reason, we unpack two of Leah's weekly plans for the children and her reported reflections on the children's responses in the next part of this chapter. These plans and reflections illustrate how Leah's planning expressed her own views of the

significance of engaging with music in daily life and how she shared this. She utilised the same approach with the adult group, but this was not formally recorded.

Music plans and reflections

Two of Leah's music plans and reflections are presented and discussed here. The
reason we present two is that the connections between the documents, recorded
one month apart, indicate the connectivity and growth that occurred from one
music session to the next. We started by asking Leah about her planning and choice
of documentation to communicate her activities to the adults of the centre.

> For planning, I use the centre curriculum document. The music concepts
> and objectives are taken from there. I plan using the curriculum document.
> I start with a warm-up, familiar teaching material, the teaching point, some
> variety – like a focused circle and other activities – and find a nice way to
> finish. I like closure. (Interview, 17 June 2008)

It is interesting to note how similar this approach is to the historical example of a
music plan provided in Chapter 1 (Champion de Crespigny, 1958). Like that example, this template tended to lead to the 'teaching point' as the third activity. Given
the importance of warming up and the confidence familiar material can provide,
this may be a pattern that remains the most suitable for music groups. Certainly, it
was a pattern Leah also used when she visited the rooms, though formal plans were
not presented on the notice board. In this section we present two music plans, Leah's
reflections and our comments. These plans and reflections would be shared with
parents and generalist teachers through display on the notice board in the corridor.
One plan each week would be presented but the different groups of children might
engage in slightly different activities. This can be seen in the reflections that provide
information across the groups.

> **MUSIC CLASS Term 2, lesson 3, date 27–8 May 2008**
> **Objectives:**
> - To develop confidence, control and awareness of singing voice
> - To develop aural awareness and skills, learning to differentiate sounds in
>   our environment and within music
> - To explore music and sound through language and story
>
> **Familiar material/warm-up:**
> - Warm-up to Egyptian music, focus on beat
> - Call and response singing
> - Make a beat, sing some low, some middle, some high
> - '*Mi Cuepo*'
> - '*Wichita Do Ya*': chant first, then sing
> - Clap rhythm with hands/drums
> - New song '*Ume-lay-la*'

Developing the language of music:
- Read *Sylvester, the Mouse with the Musical Ear*
- Ask children:
  - What were some of the country sounds he heard? What would they sound like?
  - What were some of the city sounds he heard (before he found his new home)?
  - What sound did he hear in his new home?
- Small break – stretch/movement
- Putting our musical ears on, and quietest mouse feet, we go outside and listen for what sounds we can hear
- Possibly divide into two groups for better noise levels, and reconvene to see what sounds each group heard
- Finish with familiar song

Materials and techniques:
- *Sylvester* book
- Paper and pencil for teachers
- Children's coats

Comment

This music session was designed to be more conceptual than focusing on specific musical elements. The notion of singing voice, sound awareness and meanings in music were introduced, the last through the use of story. The familiar activities involved children moving to the beat of music and also played with pitch. 'Mi Cuepo' was a song the children already knew, as they did the chant. Drums, as well as clapping, were used to explore sound and rhythm. A new song also appeared in the warm-up section. There was a suggestion that this song would become one that they would become very familiar with and be able to play with, becoming associated with musical games. In the third part of the class, Leah used a story to explore the notion of environmental sounds and the memory of sounds. The children stretched after this and played a game associated with the story; this happened outside to emphasise the environmental sounds explored earlier. The session was brought to a close by coming inside and sharing a well-known song.

This description of the session indicates how closely the objectives and the focus were connected. Leah worked with the children to develop a sense of sound memory and an awareness of different sounds. The materials needed included children's coats, which was a nice practical touch given that May can be quite cold in Melbourne.

This reflection is a general one and involved all the different children's groups. 'Ume-lay-la' was listed as a new song, but is not commented upon here. In the plan and reflection below, the children now know the song and are ready to play with it in different forms. As these sessions took place after a break, it is possible a decision was made to follow the children in their exploration of the concepts

Music with Leah..................

This week in music we focused on developing listening skills, singing and working with the beat. To warm up we danced to a piece of boppy Egyptian music, concentrating on moving different parts of our bodies on the beat and double time, using movements derived from the traditional dance that goes with this particular music. The children had some good ideas for movements for dancing on the beat, and so we alternated leaders for the duration of the song.

We then revised our Spanish song- Mi Cuepo- which many of the children remembered the words and the melody quite well. We shared another familiar song, and then learned a new one: a Native American sounding song with a catchy melody and beat, using hands to help pitch our voices. The children picked it up very quickly.

We read a section of a lovely story called- "Sylvester- the Mouse with a Musical Ear," which described several sounds that Sylvester heard in different situations. We discussed what the country sounds were in the book, what the city sounds were, and tried to produce them with our own voices. We then were very quiet, listening for sounds we could hear in our own environment. Everyone's ears were definitely tuned in, as many children picked up sounds that were not at all obvious!

To finish we played a quick music/movement game akin to musical statues, and gathered together to sing goodbye. It was lovely to see the children again after my absence.

FIGURE 4.1 Music with Leah (1)

introduced and, therefore, new material was introduced that was easy to 'pick up'. In the next example, we can see how Leah has used similar material to the previous plan, but the use of the material has grown. '*Wichita Do Ya*' is no longer a familiar warm-up song, but is being used for rhythmic expression as well as a song, and '*Ume-lay-la*', the new song in the first music session, is now a source for call and response singing.

> **MUSIC CLASS Term 2, lesson 5, date 10–11 June 2008**
> **Objectives:**
> - To learn new songs and chants while focusing on beat and rhythm
> - To distinguish singing voice and other emotions/qualities we can express through voice
> - To focus on the feeling of peace and happiness in our bodies through meditation and singing
>
> **Familiar material/warm-up:**
> - Warm-up: follow the leader, 'beat movements', try to introduce double time for different movements. Try with slower music also for contrast
> - 'Little Seed' scale song
>
> **Developing the language of music:**
> - 'Way Down South where Pineapples Grow' chant/rhyme/song
> - '*Wichita Do Ya*': rhythmic chant with body percussion. Then as song
> - '*Ume-lay-la*': African song – revise as a call-and-response word game, then sing and teach the new section
> - 'This is my … voice' game. Model more examples – fast, slow, serious/ joking, confused, frustrated, relieved … then move into high/low/ medium pitch recognition game
> - 'Light a Candle for Peace': songs and meditation
> - Introduce song – very special – about sending peace into the world
> - Lying down in own space, listening to the gentle music
> - Close eyes, and think about a time when you felt happy and peaceful: bedtime story, song, one day in the park – sun shining and beautiful butterfly. Light a candle in your hearts
> - Everyone hold their candles in the circle and sing together

Comment

Leah's objectives were ambitious, as there is a lot of material in this planned session. There was a focus on beat and rhythm, which is not unusual with this age group as children will enjoy comparing beat and rhythm. She has also added in the idea of using the voice expressively; this is quite a different focus. Leah, as she said, likes closure, so the last part of the session tended to dominate; the emotive side of the music came to the fore. The familiar material was used to introduce tempo and play with pitch. The 'teaching' part of the session was quite complex. All the objectives were connected to the activities. The first song was a simple response song the children

Music with Leah.................

This week we began with our warm up dance and the children took turns to lead us in movements they could do on the beat. We also experimented doing the movements twice as fast while keeping in time, which helped us to compare how the different rhythms feel in our bodies.

We began with a rhyming chant with actions that was familiar to some of us, focusing on using lots of expression in our voices that we had worked with last week. The children enjoy dramatising it and coordinating the different movements and rhythm. We also tried singing it as a song.

After singing a few familiar songs, we continued with our African song, learning the new section and this time bringing in the drum for accompaniment. It's quite a tricky song to learn, but the children are doing well joining in and keeping the beat as we sing. We then played a game that involved singing and identifying high, low and middle range sounds.

For some movement, we played a game of musical statues, and "find the missing somebody, which involved trying to make our movements suit the quality of the music, (if it had a strong beat, or a flowing, smooth quality, etc), listening and memory skills.

We then learned a new song, a very gentle one called "Light a Candle for Peace." To get a sense for the mood of the song, we did a meditation lying down listening to some beautiful peaceful music. We remembered a time when we felt happy and peaceful, and imagined some situations which might invoke that feeling. We imagined lighting a candle in our hearts that sent beautiful, warm golden light all throughout our bodies. We then brought our 'candles' and our peace back into the circle to learn and sing this new song. A very beautiful way to finish our music class for this week.

FIGURE 4.2 Music with Leah (2)

knew and this paved the way for African song, '*Ume-lay-la*', which was being revised as a call-and-response song. This was used to practise beat and rhythm. Before singing the African song, the children had the opportunity to move while chanting and doing body percussion. Voices and emotions were then linked to pitch and tempo. The children finished with the 'Candle for Peace' song, which brought into play the idea of heightened emotions and memory. Describing the plan indicates how clearly Leah was able to link her objectives to the implementation of the activities through-out the session, even though they seemed ambitious at the beginning.

This reflection was accompanied by two photographs. One, as described above, had the children lying in a circle with a candle of peace in the middle. The second photo showed the children playing a freezing game. They were freezing in the shape of dinosaurs demonstrating 'some shapes they saw on their trip to the museum'. The reflection is of a general nature, as this is a report of the sessions for all the different groups. The statue game was not in the original plan, but was played with the Wattles group, who had been to the museum. The music plan seemed quite didactic, but this suggests a spontaneity and ability to respond to children's immediate experiences.

Discussion of lesson plans and reflections

This discussion supports and extends the comments made above. They are based on Leah's plans and reflections from 2008. We have presented two examples a month apart to indicate how Leah slowly built on children's knowledge through repeti-tion of exercises using a variety of content, and followed the children's displayed competence to decide when to introduce new material. Leah's plans, as stated in the comments above, are impressive; a lot of the content offered was diverse in style and language and represented variety and balance of activity designed to encour-age engagement from such young children. She used many modes to interest the children, including audio, visual, whole-body movement, games, digital media, instruments, stories and rituals like 'goodbye' songs. One of the striking things in her repertoire was the idea of silence as a musical concept. This was illustrated in the June reflection, where Leah described finishing the session with the song 'Light a Candle for Peace'. The children were encouraged to go inside themselves to explore memories and feelings of happiness and peace. Coloured scarves and other materials were used to paint the music, so the children became adept at different levels of symbolic representation and layered symbol use. The move from 'familiar' to introduce 'unfamiliar' in the example plans was a common approach used throughout.

Leah's planning was systematic, uniform in the formatting and was influenced by her use of a template. Leah individualised her template by putting her name and a logo on her reflection sheet. She recalled: 'The logo is a scanned image of a felted and embroidered textile that I made, combined with drawings' (Interview, 9 June 2014). The dancing figure, the colours and the treble and bass clef combine to give an idea of Leah's eclectic style when choosing material. Her philosophy of music was strong and she sought different ways of expressing this with the children.

Her plans indicate she moved carefully from simple to more complex concepts, building up knowledge of music, as well as children's self-confidence. She was clearly aware of scaffolding; this is evidenced by the way in which she was able to spontaneously change her plans, depending on the response from the children. She planned formally and then let the children take the lead by observing them closely and being sensitive to their efforts.

The example lesson plans were one month apart and the specific connections between the two are clear. Looking from one to another, we can see that the activities offered were repeated and/or correlated. Leah started with simple echo songs and, a few weeks later, was not only planning to have children echo in a foreign language, but she was also performing call-and-response songs. In this case, '*Ume-lay-la*' was the song she was using and, from her reflections, we see that some children were finding this challenging.

> After singing a few familiar songs, we continued with our African song, learning the new section and, this time, bringing in the drum for accompaniment. It is quite a tricky song to learn, but the children are doing well joining in and keeping the beat as we sing. (Reflection, 27–8 May, 2008)

The above quote is an expression of Leah's awareness of children's developmental levels and her sensitivity to this. At the same time, she was pursuing her goals of sharing complex ideas and musical experiences with the children. She was aware of the challenging rhythms her musical repertoire could present, but, nonetheless, she persevered with exploring a diversity of music with the children and trusted them to gain from such experiences and challenges.

We commented that Leah would use ritual, such as finishing on a familiar good-bye song, but these moments were chosen purposively. Leah was flexible and made allowances for the children's responses in order to let themes or ideas emerge. An example of this was the statement, 'finish with familiar song' in the first example plan presented here, allowing for choosing a song on the spot. In contrast, the second plan described how she planned to finish with the peace candle event, which was emotive and calm but quite different from a ritualised finish. In this way, she did not become dependent on ritual for ritual's sake and used it to enhance the experience when appropriate.

As evidenced by the peace candle and her enthusiasm for group singing as a way of developing well-being, Leah believed that singing and music foster development of the 'body and soul'. Therefore, her music was not just about musical concepts, but also about a way of relating to others, of nurturing self and others and as a way of life. Her music was connected to who she felt she was and, therefore, expressed strong feelings for nature and humanity. Leah used the music to improve well-being and was promoting this use of music among the children and staff, aiming to build a nurturing, compassionate and empathetic community within the centre. This belief in community was one reason she chose to share the music across the rooms and with the staff singing group. Leah had a culturally diverse background which shaped her interests in sharing musical experiences from as wide a range of cultures as possible. She did not emphasise commonly used children's songs in her repertoire, but would use them if they served a purpose. She sought material from her own experiences and travels, but also researched sound, rhythms and languages that provided a richness and unusual quality. Repertoire was drawn from all over the world.

Leah actively used her reflections to recognise children's competence and achievements. She used praise in a meaningful manner to acknowledge genuine contributions and growth in understanding. She appreciated what the children brought to the musical space and what they offered. She was mindful of these gifts and this can be seen throughout the plans and reflections, as she often followed the children's lead. At the same time, her reflections and communications with parents were honest and she was always keen to inform them of achievements and challenges.

Conclusions

The theme that arises from Leah's approach to music, musicality and working with the children was her strong interest in diverse music and the idea that music is a cultural practice that can be a socially unifying force. Leah's work at the ELC is an example of the ever increasing interest in diversity in music. In the introduction to *Cultural Diversity in Music Education*, Campbell *et al.* (2005) comment: 'We are now witnessing the rise of community music activities and African music as major sources of learning and inspiration' (p. vi). Leah was an embodiment of this movement. She lived and breathed her music and wanted a strong musical culture to be part of everyone's experience. In her interview, she regretted that her two young nieces were not exposed to adults who engaged in music, either formally or informally, and she thought this was all too common in children's lives today. She thought that children could learn culture by watching and joining with others, and her own background and travels had given her a genuine interest in many types and styles of music. She was also very interested in improvisation. All this could be seen in her activities within the ELC and the music she chose to work with.

The diversity that Leah represented is especially significant in a country like Australia, where the population is predominantly multicultural. For children to have the opportunity to explore musical cultures, within their own early childhood cultural milieu of the centre, makes the experience richer. They are in their familiar surroundings, with their own community of friends, and are, therefore, open to risks, curious and confident to explore their own tasks and preferences. The music and materials they engaged with under Leah's tuition were intercultural and provided the potential for them to develop a broad and open-minded approach to listening and participating in musical activity. Leah's eclectic offerings also took the music sessions beyond what is commonly offered to children and moving, musically, into quite complex worlds. Community and cultural plurality were the strengths of Leah's music, especially since these two aspects of experience sum up her philosophical approach.

Another aspect of music that Leah was sensitive to was that of performance. Although the children were used to movement songs and games – it was with Lesley that the idea of public performance had developed first – Leah advanced this notion. With Lesley, the children were asked to sing at assembly. Sometimes, if the children had all learned the same song in their groups with Lesley, the entire centre would sing the song, with Lesley guiding them to sing in tune. Under Leah, musical performance became an ongoing activity. One valuable aspect of these experiences was that the children experienced performance formally at assembly. They also performed for other groups in the centre, watched their teachers and then acted out these ideas in their play lives. This musical play led to the children's chorus described in Chapter 8.

The formal and informal learning taking place would deepen children's ability to 'know' music as a childhood language. Marsh (2010), in a study carried out in primary school playgrounds, commented on the contrast between children's abilities when they were in a play situation and what they brought into the classroom. For very young children, the world of play and learning is often blurred and there is an opportunity to span new and exciting places. Leah was able to do this and it was through some of these events that took place when Leah was in the centre that the idea of the children's singing group emerged (Chapter 8).

5

YOUNG CHILDREN, MUSIC AND MUSICAL CONTENT

Introduction

In this chapter we discuss the third musician, Kylie. She was a classically trained singer whose main interest was opera; she performed in the chorus of the state opera company. Kylie had not worked formally with young children before and, therefore, sought guidance by undertaking a training programme that focused on Kodaly methods. She designed her term programme using many Kodaly elements and relied (not exclusively) on the children's songs and games in the Kodaly-based book *Catch a Song* (Hoermann and Bridges, 1989), which included songs and suggested activities around each song. Her plans and methods are described in this chapter.

The events reported on here involved Kylie's approach to young children learning music and the sessions she planned and conducted, as well as a project that occurred in the centre concurrently. This project developed from Kylie including music appreciation exercises in her weekly music sessions. One group of fifteen three- and four-year-old children, from the Eucalypt room, with their room teacher Suzana (Chapter 6), became enamoured with a prolonged exploration of Mozart's *The Magic Flute*. Kylie, a mother of young children herself, believed that young children could achieve much through music, both conceptually and technically, and she included a number of the better-known works from the classical repertoire in the music programme. Her long-term plans for the year indicated that, in her appreciation work, she would focus on the *Mother Goose Suite* (Maurice Ravel), *Carnival of the Animals* (Camille Saint-Saëns), *The Nutcracker* (Pyotr Ilyich Tchaikovsky) and *The Magic Flute* (Amadeus Mozart). These classical works were to be explored over four terms, with *The Magic Flute* listed for term one.

Although all the children in the ELC actively engaged with this music appreciation programme, it was the children in the Eucalypts group who especially liked and embraced the activities involved in their introduction to *The Magic Flute*.

This could have been influenced by the overt enthusiasm of their teacher, Suzana (Chapter 6), who became a keen protagonist in this musical project. Kylie used the Kodaly practice of moving from the known to the unknown to better explore meanings in the music she was presenting. These relationships between the familiar and unfamiliar are discussed in this chapter to illustrate Kylie's approach to the children's musical experience and how she sought to extend the experience by starting with material they could manipulate because they already had some mastery over it. An illustration of how the children used their competence to further their learning can be seen when their knowledge of language and children's literature was used to frame their understandings of the story of *The Magic Flute*.

Lesley and Leah, the first two musicians to work with the children, were aware of Kodaly and Lesley especially used some aspects of his technique when emphasising pitch through physical movements, but it was Kylie who presented the children with the most formal approach to content by stressing the formal musical literacy characteristics of the Kodaly approach. She selected content carefully to assist in the task of encouraging children to enjoy music, to become informed listeners and to be able to play with musical notation in the same way they were beginning to use number and letter symbols. We discuss Kylie's role and approach, provide examples from her long- and short-term plans, the repertoire of songs, games and music she chose for active listening. We include a discussion of the project of *The Magic Flute* as an adventure led by the children, along with their role as protagonists and participants, and conclude by discussing the provocations (Edwards, Gandini and Forman, 1998), which were drivers in the musical experiences Kylie was involved with the children, staff and parents of the centre. In the sections about Kylie and the repertoire she used, we have mainly used data from her interviews and music plans to attempt to capture her voice when describing her practices. This decision was made because Kylie followed and interpreted her teaching in a Kodaly framework and her own explanations for actions seemed the best way to present this.

The musician

Approach and role

As well as being a trained singer, Kylie had also studied and completed a degree in psychology. Music had been significant throughout Kylie's life, as she was brought up in a musical family. As a mother of two children who attended the ELC, she became interested in music education for pre-school children. When Leah left the centre to travel to South America, Kylie was approached by the centre director to become the music specialist. She took on this challenge and developed a music programme based on her personal and professional knowledge, expertise and individual beliefs about children, music and learning. She was, first and foremost, a singer, so it was appropriate that her teaching approach was strongly influenced by Kodaly, who believed that singing was the foundation for all music education and that a child could be introduced to formal musical concepts at a young age. Kylie studied the pedagogy and philosophy of Kodaly with a private educator before undertaking the music programme at the centre.

Long-term plans were developed for a whole year, with weekly lesson plans and reports presented as reflections. Both were based on the following concepts, which she termed 'elements': performing, reading, writing, creating, improvising and listening. The outcomes designed for the children 'would demonstrate their growing understanding by practising in a variety of ways and in increasingly difficult contexts' (Term I plans, 2011). Her plans indicated that children would progress from a knowledge of songs and music, using examples from their known repertoire, to examples in unknown repertoire. She used the headings listed above to arrange her sessions. The following information is taken from her long-term lesson plans for four terms. A template, 'Music with Kylie', was posted for the parents and staff on the noticeboard in the corridor each week and reflected how skills had been introduced. Pedagogically, these elements were considered to be across three levels of competence, which were labelled 'preparation', 'presentation' (make conscious) and 'practice'. Most of her long-term plans were labelled preparation or presentation, so the emphasis was on experience, then guided discovery and use of musical symbols.

Kylie's singing activities to develop 'performing' skills were progressed developmentally and included the following exercises:

a. Teacher singing *solfa* and accompanying each note with the [*solfege*] hand signs while the children echo the notes and repeat the *solfege* hand signs.
b. Teacher showing the hand signs, with the children reading the signs and singing *solfa* and then showing hand signs
c. Teacher singing with text while children echo with *solfa*
d. Teacher singing with rhythm names and children singing *solfa*
e. Teacher playing the piano and children singing *solfa*
f. Teacher humming on a neutral syllable, children singing *solfa*

Activities under the heading 'reading' included experiences such as singing a known song with *solfa* and hand signs; the notation used became progressively more detailed as listed below.

a. Reading from a stick notation
b. Reading from the staff (no stems present)
c. Reading from the staff (with stems)
d. Matching the song titles to the song notations

'Writing' exercises consisted of tasks like filling in the missing notes to a known song in stick and staff notations. In the area of 'creating', the children were encouraged to create melodic patterns to specific rhythms or ideas; for 'improvising', the children participated in games of question and answer. 'Listening' required the children to try to identify tonal patterns in musical pieces. For instance, in a section of Grieg's *Hall of the Mountain King* the children listened to the same section several times and, after the first time, put up their hand every time they heard the *so-mi* pattern.

Repertoire

Kylie planned at a number of levels. She had long-range plans, weekly plans and weekly reflections, containing reports and comments on what had actually taken place. These reflections were displayed for parents and staff and were often accompanied by photos of the children engaged in the different activities. In her folder, Kylie also had the details of songs and games she would use to introduce concepts to the children; when they had discovered elements of an activity she would further share their explorations, as well as adding more formal literacy exercises, or games. In this way, a single song or game might be valuable at a number of levels. The overall music lesson plan for the year 2012 consisted of introducing elements representative of the importance placed on pitch preparation and an awareness of beat, as well as a developmental sequence. In term one, the children were to focus on the rhythm *taa ti-ti* to a level of preparation. In term two, the *so-mi* (the falling minor third) pitch interval was introduced and *rest-saa* (i.e., use of *saa*), both vocalised and with a gesture to indicate a rest, was introduced at the end of the term. In term three, the addition of *la* to *so* and *mi* became a focus of the repertoire and also 2/4 metre. No new elements were listed for term four, so presumably this was a time for consolidation or practice.

Kylie compiled a list of songs suitable for the children's singing ranges. For instance, for teaching the *so-mi* interval, the songs were divided by their title, tone set (i.e., relating to scales), time and musical context, as well as their teaching purpose. The repertoire ranged from very simple to rather complex melodies. An example of a simple song to illustrate the *so-mi* pattern was 'Caterpillar' (Hoermann and Bridges, 1989, p. 31). This song, based on a Hungarian tune, is in 2/4 time, the key of G and has a strong *so-mi* pattern repeated for six bars. The first bar consists of four quavers, *so, so, mi, mi,* and the second consists of two quavers and a crotchet, *so, so, mi.* These two bars are repeated three times and the seventh bar has four quavers, *so, fa, me, re, do,* with the last bar culminating in two crotchets on *do.* This song was also used as a circle game; Australian words were added.

> Cat-er-pill-ar crawl-ing round,
> Try-ing not to make a sound.
> Comes a mag-pie from the sky,
> Cat-er pil-lar 'bye bye'. (Hoermann and Bridges, 1989, p. 31)

The children would crawl around on the ground like caterpillars; one child was the magpie. On the descending scale at the end of the song, the magpie would fly down and catch a caterpillar.

In her music circle games, Kylie would start with songs that emphasised melodic development of *do*, *mi*, *so*, which she used as a foundation to increase the children's musical understanding and vocabulary. The 'Caterpillar' song had strong rhythmic elements, the *so-mi* emphasis and the descending scale, which made it a rich example for her to use with the children. Another song from the same music book, also using an Australian theme to a Hungarian melody, was 'Kangaroo' (Hoermann and Bridges, 1989, p. 91). This song had the *so-mi* emphasis and descending scale, as well as a solo part, but now the solo part was sung and physically acted out. On the descending scale, one child would swoop on another child who was pretending to be a sleeping kangaroo, and sing 'Guess who's playing just for fun'. The child pretending to be the kangaroo would try to guess the name of the child singing, before opening their eyes. Kylie also used traditional songs and was happy to change words – for example, the American children's singing game 'Here Comes a Bluebird' (Hoermann and Bridges, 1989, p. 66) was changed so the children could name their favourite birds.

Kylie's planning was methodical and systematic, as were the post-session reflections that she shared with the children's families. As stated above, these reflective thoughts and music session descriptions were displayed on the parent notice board on a weekly basis. These notes were evidence of how Kylie connected the music programme with the overarching centre 'theme', as well as her strong focus on musical forms and elements within the music sessions. An example of this was a theme being pursued in 2011. The centre was studying the idea of forests during the term and, hence, in one music session, Kylie invited the children to compose forest music. The children used the piano, as well as drawing trees, wind, a pond, birds, snakes and flowers; they created a story of forest sounds. The children combined the two elements of the sounds from the piano and their drawings into a composition and wrote it down. Some children even used notation to express their parts of the music. They then chose the instruments they thought would best suit the sounds and Kylie conducted the completed composition. This is how she reported it to the parents in her weekly reflection.

> The children composed their own forest music and chose instruments to accompany the story their music told. For example, there were instruments that represented rain, wind rustling old leaves, emus, baby kookaburras in their nest, bushes with berries and spiders in webs. Each group chose their own title – for example, the Eucalypts chose *A Deep Dark Forest* (23 September 2011).

As well as music appreciation, Kylie planned more formal listening activities, using the same classical music. The four pieces of classical music listed earlier were a continuing thread across the four terms of the year. Recorded copies of the music for each term were given to the home-room educators to extend children's familiarity with the music and their awareness of the possibilities of the music – to help them become educated listeners. Through her reflections Kylie shared this strategy with the parents: 'We revisited Ravel's *Mother Goose Suite*, listening to 'Tom Thumb'. Each room now has a copy of Ravel's *Mother Goose Suite* and excerpts from Tchaikovsky's ballet of *Sleeping Beauty*, which is what we have been listening to in class' (Reflection, 19 May 2011).

Exploration of particular ideas was varied and detailed. To prepare for a visit to a symphony orchestral concert she decided to introduce the children to the participants of the orchestra and the roles they played.

> We discussed conducting today. We discussed conducting and how important it is for there to be someone who keeps all the instruments of an orchestra working together. Everyone had a turn at conducting music with a straw baton in 2/4, 3/4 or 4/4 time. We then watched a conductor working with an orchestra playing Smetana's *Die Moldau*, which we had listened to before – this time we watched from the conductor's viewpoint.
>
> Everyone then walked, skipped and stomped around the room with their batons, keeping time with several contrasting pieces of music. We listened to excerpts of the 'Promenade' from Mussorgsky's *Pictures at an Exhibition*, Strauss's *Blue Danube*, Prokofiev's *Peter and the Wolf* and Aaron Copland's *Appalachian Springs*. We had to listen really hard because sometimes the tempo and the dynamics changed.
>
> We finished our session by having some quiet time on the floor, listening to the lark in the sky in Vaughn Williams's *Lark Ascending*. Some children thought the lark was flying up high, then away down low, swooping, landing in a tree and singing. (Reflections, 17 August 2011)

Listening was a strategy to support centre themes. The nearby Yarra river was a favourite place for the children to visit and Kylie contrasted this very brown, comparatively little river with different views of rivers through musical interpretation.

> We listened to a symphonic poem by Smetana about the river Vltava (*Die Moldau*). Smetana uses tonal painting to describe the course the Vltava takes from the Austrian Alps, through the picturesque countryside of the Czec Republic, past ancient castles, palaces, farmland and villages, past the capital city of Prague, till it joins the river Elbe and runs into the sea. Within the music can be heard the bubbling of a small brook, as it transforms into a river, a wedding dance taking place on the river bank, dancing of the mermaids in the moonshine and fast rapids. As we were listening, we discussed the similarities (autumn trees, swans, bridges and towns, the brown colour of the rivers) and the differences (we have no castles, palaces and our river is not as vast). (Reflections, 20 July 2011)

This Yarra River was a special space for the children of the centre and has appeared in most of the chapters of this book. As well as the above listening experience, the river was also a way of linking into local indigenous knowledge and Australian themes. Such a lens would fit well with Kodaly's beliefs about music and folk language:

> connecting into Aboriginal Elder Uncle Larry's visit last week, we turned the dreamtime story of *Tiddalik, the Frog* into a musical poem. Using various instruments and visual cues for the river, we journeyed through the Tiddalik landscape, from frog sounds and bubbling water to the many Australian animals that tried to make Tiddalik laugh. (Reflections, 22 November 2010)

Kylie's approach to her music sessions was content-focused and, therefore, her own words and comments have been used as much as possible in this chapter to describe what was happening. Kylie had style and the sessions were lively, with the children actively joining in. What struck the observers was how content-heavy these plans were. Expectations of children were extremely high and they rose to the challenge. There was also space for those who exercised the right to be more watchful than active participants. In the next section of this chapter, we discuss the children's engagement with *The Magic Flute*, which was part of the music session that Kylie used to encourage music appreciation. In keeping with Kodaly ideas, children moved through stages of understanding (pre-conscious, conscious and creative). Kylie used these categories in her plans to refer to children becoming familiar with a piece of music, which she viewed as preparation for active involvement, including listening. The conscious stage of exploration would lead to a more expert engagement that would enable 'active listening'. After this stage, the children would be able to use the familiar material in an experimental and possibly creative way.

The Magic Flute project

When Kylie decided to introduce the children to classical music, she chose *The Magic Flute* as the first piece of music the children would become familiar with. Kylie introduced the opera via online streaming and showed the children the recording produced by the New York Metropolitan Opera (Taymor, 2010). To help the children gain an understanding of the story as a whole, she also used two picture story books produced for children (Gatti, 1997; Greaves, 1989). This fairy tale stirred the children's imaginations and captured their interest for more than eight weeks. The 'movies', as children referred to *The Magic Flute* as they watched it as a serial, took place in the gallery, with an overhead projector (connected to a PC), for about twenty minutes each week. Kylie made sure that a cinema-like atmosphere was created by switching the lights off and pulling the blinds down. Relationships between familiar events (the literary exploration of a book) with unfamiliar experiences (watching an opera as a serial) gave the children's activities depth and there was an atmosphere of excitement.

The story had been made accessible to children through picture story books (Gatti, 1997; Greaves, 1989; Teis, 2008) and the Metropolitan Opera (Taymor, 2010) family-friendly film version of the story and music. This Taymor production of the opera was considered exciting and the children could enjoy the fantasy with kite puppets, animal imagery and masks, together with a set filled with geometric shapes and sculptures. The effects in the performance were simple, but strong enough to give the children feelings of vicarious fright and anxiety for their favourite characters. Papageno was the overall favourite and the children were often concerned for him. The serpent in the opening scene could be seen to be a row of dancers holding tall sticks that held up the puppet monster as it swerved and flew across the stage. The three wise spirits, who serve as guides to Prince Tamino, floated across the stage, perched on a huge flying bird. The children found the puppetry entrancing and one child asked, having watched the puppet bears dance across the stage, 'How do you make a bear look like a butterfly?' (Nyland et al., 2013). This step of increasing complexity is a sequence that appears in most of Kylie's weekly music plans. In terms of The Magic Flute, reading and discussing the picture story book led to the children following the music and songs of each character of the opera and anticipating what would unfold each week in their movie serial. The Magic Flute lived outside the music room as the characters like the Queen of the Night and Papageno began to feature in the children's dramatic play, while at home some children watched YouTube versions of some of the songs, especially the 'Queen of the Night'; some enjoyed CD recordings with their parents. The pictorial and detailed drawings of the story, done by the children (Figures 5.1–5.5), are indicative of the enthusiasm and connections that the children found in this opera.

During the preparation for the initial showing of The Magic Flute, Kylie discussed the quality of sound that the flute made and the children listened to recordings of flute music and commented on the sound. Initially, Kylie had been going to read the story and show a little of the film to the children; it was in the second week, when the children demanded more of the 'movie', that it became obvious this event had the potential to become more than a listening exercise. Below is an example of Kylie's notes to parents as they were presented on the notice board. The template Kylie used had the same format as that used by Lesley and Leah and, like them, she individualised the form in her own way. One aspect of Kylie's reflections on the music sessions that distinguished her plans from the others was the inclusion of a quote each week. In the example presented, there are connections between the musical content of the first part of the session and The Magic Flute viewing that followed these activities. Kylie was working with the idea of performance and audience, as well as high and low voices. This was the first time the children had seen Sarastro and, as they already felt that the Queen of the Night must be a good person 'because of her beautiful clothes', she wanted them to be receptive to Sarastro's deep voice when he appeared. From the records cited below, this was a successful strategy.

Rhythm and melody

Music with Kylie

'Music washes away from the soul the dust of everyday life'
Berthold Auerbach (1812–1882)
Monday, 8 November 2010
Focusing on rhythm work, we started music today singing and playing the claves for 'Somebody's Knocking on my Window' and then listening and copying rhythms for 'Let's play a game that's lots of fun, listen to this rhythm and pass it on'.

We then moved onto singing a favourite, 'Goanna Lying in the Midday Sun', adding a 'frill neck lizard' with a slurping vocal warm-up. To explore the concept of audience and performance, we divided into two groups, alternating one group watching the other group singing and dancing 'I am an Aussie Rosella'. We also practised bowing at the end of the performance while the audience clapped. Using the xylophone for an accompaniment, we explored singing 'I'm a Little Bat' as a call-and-response song.

In *The Magic Flute* and singing today, we listened to the voices different characters have. The Queen of the Night and Pamina have very high voices, whereas Sarastro, the king, has a very deep voice; Papageno and Tamino have more medium voices, according to the children. We felt our voices vibrate and resonate by lightly touching our throats while humming.

The music programme explored a number of musical concepts with a rich repertoire and selected songs that enhanced the children's understanding of singing in different pitch, voice-type, rhythm, words and sounds. She wanted the children to examine a range of voices and to explore how they contributed to the building up of characters in the plot of the opera. To keep families informed, Kylie started writing 'Excerpts from the Opera' and including these on the notice board with her plans and reflections.

Excerpts from Act 1
Papageno sings: 'I am Papageno, that's my name.'
Papageno sings about his job as a bird-catcher and adds that he is also trying to catch a sweetheart! He is a happy-go-lucky fellow, not particularly heroic, and his human feelings get him into all sorts of trouble. Despite himself, he rescues a princess, undergoes trials of courage and wins a girl of his own in the end.
The children identify with joyful/not so brave but willing to give it a try aspect of Papageno. They identify with the 'child of nature' part of him, that he just likes to eat and play and that his bravado sometimes leads him into trouble.
Prince Tamino sings: 'This image is enchantingly beautiful.'
As soon as he sees the portrait of Pamina, Tamino is enthralled and bursts into ardent song, expressing his love and longing to see her and have her with

him always. I asked the children to imagine they were singing this song to someone they really loved and they sat enthralled.

The notes describe the Queen of the Night as a passionate, otherworldly dark force, with a high soprano voice full of elaborate ornamentation, who tells Tamino in the aria 'O Tremble Not, My Dear Son' not to be afraid and that he is wise and noble and that she, a sorrowful mother, needs his help. 'At first this aria is slow, sad and gentle, telling of a mother's grief; it then gives way to a more intense, faster pace as she enlists Tamino's help and promises him that he will be united with Pamina.'

Kylie's records pointed out that when the children met Sarastro for the first time they 'marvelled' at his beautiful voice singing the legato lullaby-sounding aria 'Iris and Osiris'. They also became fascinated with the ordeals of silence and patience that Tamino and Papageno go through, and this brought about an animated discussion. Kylie described 'patience' as waiting without complaining and trusting that things will turn out all right. The children established that patience 'looks like when you are hungry and waiting for Mum or Dad to serve you dinner' or 'when you planted some vegetables and are waiting for them to grow' or 'when someone is playing with your favourite toy and you let them play,'cause it's your turn soon'. These associations, so well verbalised by the children, were the result of the provocations the children encountered as they explored Mozart's story and music.

The children as participants

The children in Suzana's room, the Eucalypt group of children, had group discussions, facilitated by Suzana after many of the music sessions. One activity was to create large collaborative drawings of the opera characters. Below are some examples of these drawings and comments made by the children during discussion (Figures 5.1–5.5). These are indicative of the children's deep interest in the topic of the opera, the music, the story and the people in it.

The following are some of the comments made by the children and recorded by Suzana (see Chapter 6 for further discussion).

> L: The three bears are puppets made of silk, the silk moves like waves. Their claws are made of cardboard. They're hard.

The teacher noted here that L was emphasising the materials and visual aesthetics in his expressed view of the bears. He has also made a technical comment about the silk and has identified this as a means by which the puppet bears look as though they have wings.

> M. Bears are dancing with nice movements; they look like butterflies flying around.

FIGURE 5.1 Children's drawing of Papageno

M has noticed the movement and also picked up on the original comment about the butterfly.

> A. The dance made my heart break.

The teacher noted this as an emotional response to the bears. It is worth mentioning that, following a comment about 'my heart breaking' by a child in an earlier week, references to hearts became popular.

> L. (changing the subject) Papageno came down the ladder, but there was nobody on the stage holding him. They were just fixed there. (He then returned to the bears commenting they could 'go faster'.)

The teacher once again identified L's interest in the techniques or mechanics of the opera. The 'go faster' comment she surmised as possibly an emotionally charged response.

The children then commented on the prince, saying, 'He looks as if he's made out of white bone' and 'The Queen of the Night sings in a slow and beautiful voice that melts.'

'The Queen of the Night'

FIGURE 5.2   Children's drawing of the Queen of the Night

The reference to the 'white bone' was labelled visual expression and the auditory nature of R's description of the Queen's voice was noted here.

Conclusions

Provocations

Provocations are used to inspire a journey of discovery; it can be transient or a long-term investigation. A provocation is an idea, question, discussion, observation or an event that engages children's thinking. It can come from teachers, parents, the children or the wider community. The idea of provocation comes from the Reggio Emilia approach to early childhood education, but it can occur any time when working with young children, whether Reggio Emilia-inspired or not. In the ELC where Kylie was working, the Reggio Emilia approach was popular and staff members were encouraged to challenge children through thoughtful questioning, interesting walks by the river and the joy of using high-quality materials for self-expression. Major provocations that occurred while Kylie was providing musical experiences for the children were her use of Kodaly-based activities and

FIGURE 5.3 Sarastro

The Magic Flute project generally (which involved many provocations). Two subsets of this project were the use of technology, especially YouTube, and the exploration of the fairy story.

The influence of Kodaly in the centre was apparent in the work of the three musicians and might have instigated the director's move to employ specialists for the music programme, as one tenet of the Kodaly philosophy is that musicians should teach music. Kylie's take on Kodaly was fairly doctrinaire and, as indicated above, her plans followed the form of a basic lesson plan with beginning (pitch and rhythm), primary focus, change of pace, secondary focus and conclusion. The secondary focus of the session was often used as a time to have exercises that enhanced the original conceptual focus and allowed the children time for practice with familiar material, an important strategy in the Kodaly method. In this case, the story book was one artefact Kylie introduced to achieve this aim, after introducing the children to the musical concepts that would be encountered when watching the film of *The Magic Flute*. Indeed, the room teacher, Suzana, wrote in her notebook after one such session:

> The teacher finished her notes for the day with another question: 'What is it that leaves the biggest impact on each individual child: visual, auditory,

FIGURE 5.4 Pamina

narrative or technical?' I would suggest that these children were within the narrative, because of the use of the book, and therefore able to address aspects of the opera with much more depth than if they had been novices to *The Magic Flute*.

Suzana thought, therefore, that the strategy of reading the story to the children had served as a provocation to address the meaning of the whole. The children were able to explore different editions of *The Magic Flute*, retold for young children as picture story books, and discuss which version they liked the best. Teis (2008) was the decided favourite, though there were a few who enjoyed the more theatrical style of drawings in the Gatti (1997) book; the Greaves book (1989), with its more delicate pictures and pieces of music, did not attract attention. Therefore, the book the children could relate to most easily was the one that was most representative of design created for young children – clear, simple pictures with black lines, bright colours and minimal words on each page. The children used this literary version to explore the intricacies of the story.

YouTube was also a valuable provocation used to expand the children's explorations of *The Magic Flute*. Watching the production of *The Magic Flute* did reach out

One of the 'Happy Dancing Bears' by the Eucalypts

FIGURE 5.5 How do you make a bear look like a butterfly?

to these children. They engaged with the new material and their interest in Mozart was so great that, at the end of the second music session, two of the girls called out for 'the movie'. Although the ELC utilised digital technology on a daily basis, this opera was a provocation to these three- and four-year-old children, who proceeded to explore the whole opera, formally, as a serialised form of a performance; in their dramatic play; and at home, as many watched YouTube clips with their parents and grandparents. Watching at home on YouTube was an interesting way of connecting the centre and the home. One child watched with her grandfather and was able to assure the other children, when events seemed to be frightening, that all would be OK. One quite astounding result was a child who taught herself the first part of the aria of the Queen of the Night, an extraordinary, nimble melody characterised by large melodic leaps. She was able to perform this for her friends at the centre and had listened to as many versions as she could to compare the singers in the role in terms of voice colour and clothes (Nyland *et al.*, 2011). YouTube accessibility

provided a special provocation, where children could develop refined skills in critical analysis, share knowledge with their families and have their own theories about
the story and characters of *The Magic Flute*.

The Magic Flute, as a fairy story, was an excellent provocation to inspire learning
and discovery on a number of levels. A 'once upon a time' story, where the events
unfold quickly, includes a protagonist, in the form of Papageno, as a linking thread
throughout. Even Papageno's song, written in a folk style, was accessible and the
children were able to learn the song. The magic number of three, much loved in
folk and fairy stories, is present in the three tasks, the three ladies and the three boys.
Bruner (1991) discusses the power of narrative; this was a story that the children
could interpret for myriad meanings. Bruner commented on the idea of conceptualising reality and says that 'cultural products, like language and other symbolic
systems, mediate thought and place their stamp on our representations of reality'
(p. 3). He calls this 'distributed intelligence' and says it must always be seen as a
combination of the person within a context of surrounding textual supports, like
knowledge and access to a variety of literacies, and relationships that help to mentor
cultural understandings. Bruner is interested in the question of how narrative is a
mental tool that is used to construct reality. Ten features of narrative are identified
and many of these are strongly represented in a story with folk-tale elements like
The Magic Flute. These features include the use of time. Two stories, for instance, take
place simultaneously when Papageno goes into the palace and meets Pamina while
Tamino goes to the temple. One of the books the children were introduced to
contained the magic word 'meanwhile' (Greaves, 1989). Another (Gatti, 1997) had
each part of the story appearing on a double page so the reader would know that
the next page would provide another aspect of events occurring at the same time.
Teis (2008) was more linear in her approach, which made the story easier for young
children to recount. Such devices are important and exciting as children become
aware of complex notions that they can vicariously enjoy through imagination.
There are other examples of fairy-story elements found in *The Magic Flute*. Its story
is intergenerational, it is an adventure-rescue tale, a morality story, it contains many
examples of dualism – like good and evil, wise and simple, rich and poor – and
there are many rudiments of magic. It is through stories that children gain an intuitive sense of the complexity of human relationships and become competent users of
language and other symbol systems. Shank and Berman (2002) suggest that all stories are didactic in some way as they are designed to help us understand and interpret the world. All contain a sequence of events and have a structure of beginning,
middle and end. Children in the pre-school years can comprehend this narrative
structure and are ready to play with the story content by manipulating elements of
time, agency, narration and readership (Harris, 2008). The Kodaly influence was
strong in this centre and Kylie, who had trained in the Kodaly method, applied it
precisely, so this use of fairy story, children's picture books, music and in-depth
exploration of experience was very fitting. Fairy stories are a rich source of narrative
to explore with young children, given they are so grounded in cultural and historical context as well as sharing meta-themes because they have been borrowed

between cultures, changed across the centuries and because of their history of coming from oral traditions. These are stories that do not belong to one group. There are those who also have surmised that fairy stories, because of their adult themes, are socially and psychologically attractive to children (e.g., Bettelheim, 1989). The plot in *The Magic Flute* is a clear battle between good and evil, though there was some confusion for the children who did not find the Queen of the Night's clothing fitted their ideas of 'bad'. There was the presence of magic to support a happy ending for Tamino and Pamina, and good luck for the everyman Papageno.

Each of the music specialists brought something new to the programme at the ELC and Kylie's commitment to content gave new insight into children's competence. These events suggest a rhetorical question: what could be enjoyed, explored and achieved when expectations were high, content was exciting and children were respected for what they brought to the encounter?

6

AN EARLY CHILDHOOD EDUCATOR

Introduction

Suzana was an early childhood teacher with more than 25 years of experience working with young children. Music had always had a significant place in her education programmes for young children. She came from a musical family, had learned piano and violin as a child and remembered singing with her father as one of her pleasurable childhood memories. She would share these memories by singing these songs of her childhood to her colleagues in the ELC staff room. This room was large, with food preparation facilities on one side, a large table in the middle and a row of computers running along the wall opposite the food area. Suzana completed her early childhood teacher training in Europe and felt there had been a great emphasis on music in her training course in Croatia that had equipped her well for including music in her plans with the children she taught. She had completed her Graduate Diploma in Early Childhood Education and felt that the music preparation she had received was more in-depth than in Australian teacher training programmes. In her interview (14 June 2008), she stated she 'absolutely love[d] singing' and that she sang with the children and regularly used musical instruments. She was used to encouraging musicians to work with her and the children and, in a centre where she had previously worked, she had been able to collaborate with parents. Among the parents at that centre, there were some who played piano, violin and cello and visited the centre to share their expertise. In her current position, Suzana had embraced the idea of the teachers' singing group (Chapter 7), saying she found it not only beneficial for teachers, but also for the children and their families. She herself had always felt that singing could be uplifting. Suzana was an experienced kindergarten teacher and had actively contributed to developing approaches to children's education within this research centre. She had also continued to study, displaying a commitment to lifelong learning and had completed a Master of Education thesis: 'The poetical understanding of children's imagery of nature: how is poetical understanding evident in children's art?' This enthusiasm for nature, poetry and children's art was evident in the research described here. Suzana was able to integrate children's musical experiences into the home-room programme and children's spontaneous play.

In this chapter, we present Suzana as an example of a teacher/researcher who regularly attended conferences and had published her own research on children's learning and experiences. To collect data for her documentation of children's learning, she encouraged discussions, questioning on a high level, drama and visual expression through painting and drawing on an individual and group basis with the children. She recorded these initiatives as both research into children's learning and a record of the children's competence and potential. The quality of the children's work produced under her mentorship was outstanding. Examples of children's art works, from Suzana's groups, have been presented in Chapter 5 (Figures 5.1–5.5) and include children's drawings of the characters in *The Magic Flute* and the composition of the song, 'Eucalypts of Melbourne' (Chapter 7). This chapter describes the potential of the generalist teacher as a collaborator and protagonist who initiated, supported and actively participated in a range of arts activities, especially playing a lead support role in the specialist music programme. Data is drawn from interviews, observations, participant observations, examples of children's work, documentation of the projects, discussions and field notes.

Collaborative participation

Suzana was actively committed, through her own personal and educational philosophy, to the idea of community involvement. She was committed to working collaboratively and had been involved in a number of community projects within the centre. An example of a long-term project that grew out of her own personal interest and enthusiasm was a partnership she developed with a local artist who worked with glass. Suzana was strongly attracted to the craft of working with glass as an artistic medium. Approaching the artist, who was well known for his glass studio, which was within easy walking distance to the ELC, she initiated a project that, over a period of six years, involved more than 200 pre-school children from the centre. Each year the glass collaboration took its provocation from the United Nations International Year theme, which always had an environmental focus, thus simultaneously supporting two interests. The children participated in an exhibition that contained glasswork from the artist, the children's own designs for the glass, their own paintings on glass and their representations of the glass work in other mediums, such as clay. The collection of art displayed reflected the children's responses to caring for the natural world. It embodied the collective memories and experiences of the children, artists and teachers involved in this unique project. The collection, titled *Step Gently On this Earth and this Sky*, was featured in an exhibition in an art gallery in Wagga Wagga, a regional city in rural New South Wales, and attracted some media attention (Early Learning Centre, 2014).

Suzana joined the staff of the ELC when the second and third musicians, Leah and Kylie, were working with the children. She responded enthusiastically to the music component of the arts specialisation in the centre, but initially found that there was little connection between the music room and the home-rooms. The second musician, Leah, agreed with her about this. Leah wanted there to be more contact across the centre through the music programme, but, nevertheless, acknowledged that the designated music space in the gallery was something she could enjoy as an aesthetic space. 'This space! I love it. There is a beautiful presence here. The shelves, the instruments on display, the piano. Use of space for movement' (interview with Leah, 14 June 2008). On the relationship between the music sessions and the programme in the rooms she stated, 'I would like to feel more involved in the children's lives here. There is a separation of the music classes from the rooms. It would perhaps be nice to follow through into the rooms' (interview, 14 June 2008).

Leah and Suzana shared the view that singing was uplifting, a way for the adult to connect to others, to the children and even to the past, to themselves when they were children. They shared an enjoyment of a repertoire that included music from around the world. Suzana had grown up in Europe, enjoyed the folk music of her youth, engaged in *Bhajan* singing on Saturdays and took pleasure in introducing mandala/Sanskrit songs to the children. Leah, the music specialist, shared a love of folk songs, with some knowledge of Hungarian music, and had played drums and sung with groups in Egypt and South America. She also enjoyed traditional English songs like 'Oh Poor Bird' and introduced part-singing and companion songs to the singing group. These culturally diverse musical tastes gave Suzana and Leah common ground that meant they were sympathetic collaborators.

The teachers' singing group, led by Leah, gave Suzana the opportunity and support to sing around the centre all day, every day and she had thoroughly enjoyed this. The idea of the staff singing together had come simultaneously from the director and Leah and was conceived as a research project. The director suggested that the practices and performance be recorded and the staff perceptions of the experience be ascertained through interviews before and after the event. Leah thought that the singing group would not have happened so quickly and with such immediate support if it had not been set up as research, but hoped in the future such activities might become part of the culture of the centre. Suzana was enthusiastic about the music Leah brought to the centre, including her work with the staff singing group; she took longer to connect with the next music specialist, but when she did there was a noticeable change in some of her teaching practices and this was evidenced in her documentation of the content of the music sessions and her increased role as a collaborator.

The third musician, Kylie, initially had a more overtly didactic approach to her music than the previous music specialists. She was a trained opera singer and had a firm belief in the necessity of training in basic skills. Her sessions were meticulously planned and Suzana was not sure of her role at first. However, when Kylie started to unpack her ideas, Suzana was open to the notion that there had to be some adaptation to different musical preferences, beliefs about children's learning, content of music sessions and how the sessions were organised. She, thus, became an integral part of many of Kylie's initiatives.

In the next two sections of this chapter, we describe Suzana's documentation of two projects: one with the second musician, Leah, and the other with the third musician, Kylie. We also discuss her own role in these activities and her ability to support, engage and take on the role of an intentional teacher. Intentional teaching is one of eight elements of practice listed in the national Australian curriculum (DEEWR, 2009) and is described as 'deliberate, purposeful and thoughtful' (p. 15). Suzana actually identifies in her documentation times when she felt she had engaged in intentional teaching. An example was recorded in 2010, when Suzana had taken the theme of identity to explore with the children. She mixed the children's displays of spontaneous self-awareness with deliberately planned provocations and teacher-led activities. This latter she labelled intentional teaching. The children were exploring their own characteristics through story and art work and Suzana introduced 'sense of place' as part of their identity. This involved emphasising the river next to the ELC. The river and its environment was always an important thread at the centre. In this instance, Suzana helped the children create a river of silk, where they 'played' with ideas of ripples, currents and a storm. She did this mainly through singing, different rhythms and dynamics, and wrote 'intentional teaching' under the activity plan (Table 6.1), an indication that her approach was influenced by the notion of intentional teaching at this time.

Pedagogical documentation and changing relationships

The ELC was inspired by the early childhood education approach from Reggio Emilia and pedagogical documentation is an important part of the Reggio Emilia approach. Early childhood education traditionally has been based on 'child study' and recorded observations, with their accompanying interpretations a major part of early childhood teacher training programmes. This foundation idea has been developed in Reggio Emilia to encompass the role of the teacher as one of researcher. Using observations as research is a methodology that has been part of early childhood teaching. Observing is considered a reciprocal activity, by which both parties learn by the process. So, conceptualising 'pedagogical documentation as teacher research calls upon the teacher not to know with certainty but instead to wonder, to inquire with grace into some temporary state of mind and feeling in children' (Wien, Guyevskey and Berdoussis, 2011, n.p.).

Documentation is used to make learning visible and, like the children of Reggio Emilia, Suzana used many visual arts methods, as well as questioning and verbal theorising, to explore the music projects the children were involved in. In the next two sections of this chapter, two of the books Suzana developed are discussed.

These contain records of projects conducted by the second musician, Leah, and another managed by musician number three, Kylie – projects that have been referred to in other chapters of this book. These books are referred to as curriculum books at the centre, and are significant documents, reflecting each teacher's particular approaches and style of documentation. The format Suzana chose for her curriculum book, or pedagogical documentation, was an A3 format (29.7cm by 40cm), a wide format that suited her style of thinking and documentation. The books were carefully crafted. Multiple visual stimuli and prompts were utilised to assist in the narrative she was telling. She included copies of children's work that had been reduced and photocopied, photographs, typed plans cut out and pasted in and comments (including children's comments) were recorded directly into the book by hand. Hand-drawn links were used to map or web ideas and unusual visual features included a strip of film on one page. If it enhanced the effect, paper folding was used. In the book from 2008, patterned mandala representations appear frequently, often cut from magazines, and seemed to have more a decorative role, or possibly acted as a philosophical reminder to maintain a focus. This interest in the cosmos and the metaphysical can also be linked to Suzana's scholarly interest in children's art, nature and poetical understanding. It also helps to explain the central role the nearby river plays. By 2010 the mandala images were less frequent and the visual adventures in the second curriculum book were more elaborate.

The documentation in the two curriculum books varied greatly and indicated Suzana's growing skills at documentation, as well as evidencing her ability to observe, interpret and theorise and to encourage children to do the same. Her provocations were often fanciful and inspired the children to imagine multiple possibilities. For example, when exploring *The Magic Flute*, Suzana came across a postcard picture of Mozart sitting in front of a computer. She brought this in to share with the children and the responses included such ideas as a suggestion that Mozart might live in outer space. In the following section we discuss the role of pedagogical documentation as it reflects the changing relationships of musicians, Suzana as generalist teacher, music in the general programme and the specialist music programme from the studio.

Suzana's documentation and the curriculum books

Suzana kept curriculum books to record all her activities with the children and there is a large pile of these kept at the centre. The curriculum books belong to the centre, presumably because they are rich and detailed depictions of children's experiences. These books were meticulously prepared. The two examples discussed here are for 2008 and 2010, as these were the years that the Antarctica project, The Icy Land of Secrets (2008) and *The Magic Flute* project (2010) took place. Running throughout the books is the theme that Suzana had initiated relating to the glass studio. The documentation in these books is a combination of the projects occurring, the children's individual and group interests and explorations, Suzana's own plans for extending the children in the everyday and the children's responses to her

TABLE 6.1 Planned objectives, February 2008

Week 4–8 February 2008

OBJECTIVES
- For the children to become aware of and respect the similarities and differences that exist between individuals
- For children to develop the sense of belonging
- For the children to engage in the long-term project of *L'Eta Verde* by exploring and creating their visions of possible realities through their art and narratives

NEW DISCOVERIES AND LEARNING
- Exploring Antarctica: colours in the landscape, fauna, geographical terms, real and imaginary explorations through imagination and science
- Light box transparencies: glass, ice, silk, tissue paper, mirrors (the notion of fragile)
- Forms of icebergs: hard-edged, fold, crumpled, soft-edged (experimenting with paper forms)
- Imaginary journeys: going on many trips to imaginary lands, the feel of the place, time travel, the sense of belonging

provocations through a variety of languages. The children's responses and questions play an important role in these recordings of experience. Suzana's documentation changed over time and became more complex and layered. Her relationship with the music from the studio changed and, for Suzana, music became a more collaborative endeavour.

First, we describe Suzana's documentation from 2008 and the relationship of the music in the room and the music in the music space in the gallery. In the 2008 curriculum book, Suzana linked her observations closely to the project in the centre, as well as having general objectives for the children. This suggests a somewhat linear relationship between the room and the music project. The records in the curriculum book focus on the Antarctica project, which seems to become a vehicle for instigating general weekly plans. At the beginning of the term of the Antarctica project, these were the ideas for the first teaching week in February.

Ways of exploring Antarctica, described as 'windows for learning' are listed as: mindscapes for mystery and beauty; science scapes for facts, sense of place and time; time-scapes for space, time and future; metaphorical landscapes for venturing beyond the known; landscapes for impressions of the earth; sound scapes to enhance creative learning; and inscapes for mental landscapes. At this stage, the language of music is not strongly emphasised, although Suzana introduces a lot of musical language through poetry and wordplay. An example is the following story written by Suzana and the children.

> *The Iceberg's Heart*
> At the bottom of the big, big world, there is an iceberg called Melt (Child B).
> He had a blue heart, as blue as the sea (Child TT).

Melt always dreamed of seeing his heart, but he couldn't. His heart was deep down inside his body of ice (Child G).

One day he asked a group of penguins if they could dive into the frozen ocean and find his heart (Child S).

The penguins went searching deep and deeper, and on the bottom of the snow mountains of the ocean they spotted a blue, blue, shiny love heart (Child J).

They couldn't pick it up, because Melt's heart was made out of blue ice. It was frozen and heavy, too heavy for them to pick it up (Child S).

So, after good thinking, the penguins asked some friendly seals if they could help and flip it up with their strong tails (Child E).

But the seals couldn't do it – the heart was just too big (Child H).

Both penguins and seals swam back onto the surface of the ocean and they told Melt, 'Your heart is just too heavy, we can't lift it up.' (Child R).

'But we can tell you that your heart is blue as the sea and the sky. It is covered with beautiful diamond dust and it is everywhere in the ocean.' (Child S).

The iceberg called Melt liked what they said. (Child B).

He felt his heart shimmering. It made all of the Antarctica beautiful. (Children J and S)

This story is an example of the collaborative work that Suzana often did with the children. In this case, she has used the format of a group time on the mat; this activity often occurred after music sessions. She would help the children explore their feelings and ideas, by combining her own prompts (pre-prepared challenge questions, artefacts, citations of the children's own reflective comments, as well as games and stories) to remind the children about what they already knew and to encourage imaginative flights. Ice, melting, penguins and sea lions had all been objects of interest for the children, as well as the idea that you cannot climb inside an iceberg because it might roll over. The song 'Diamond Dust' had become a signature tune.

Has an iceberg got a heart? This was one of the questions the children put to staff at Casey Station, in Antarctica, as part of the project. The staff at Casey Station had become more creative in the way they had crafted their answers to children's questions and how they explained the Antarctic images they shared with the children over the time of this particular undertaking. From fairly factual descriptions of penguin colonies and whale sizes, the answers to the children's questions about icebergs became more imaginative. The staff at the station also became more collaborative, as a number of members of the scientific research group in Antarctica contributed to replying to the children. The answer to the question about the iceberg heart is an example.

This is a tricky one. I've gone and asked all the other people here and they say; 'Of course the iceberg has a heart.' One person said: 'An iceberg has a heart because it is always blue. Did you know when you break a bit off an iceberg it is filled with bubbles and when you drop it into water it fizzes as if it is filled with life. To have life you have to have a heart. Water is the blood of the world, so maybe Antarctica's icebergs can provide the world with fresh drinking water into the future. I think an iceberg has to have a heart and probably a soul. It is certainly worthy of one.' (Deans, 2008)

Such rich material led to activities like the jointly authored story about 'Melt', which were all carefully and aesthetically noted by Suzana. The curriculum book for 2008 is excellent pedagogical documentation that comprises a number of mapping techniques, largely using linguistic and visual forms of expression, to illustrate Suzana and the children's knowledge, learning and theorising. The presence of music in the 2008 curriculum book, however, is less visible than it was in the 2010 book. There is a mention of sound scapes and the poem 'Diamond Dust' does appear, written into the middle of a diamond shape that contains suggestions, on each side of the diamond, of the children's expressive activities in relation to dramatic storytelling, creative expression, metaphor and aesthetics. Although music is less visible in the 2008 documentation, it certainly was present in the daily programme. Suzana commented on her use of music at this time:

> Yes, I sing all the time – e.g., gathering time, meditation time, while we pack up, form celebrations. We use instruments – e.g., this morning the work experience student made frog sounds with the children. The children love the mandala/Sanskrit songs. If we didn't have access to the specialist music programme I would probably do more. (Interview, 14 June 2008)

By the time the third musician, Kylie, was teaching in the programme there was a distinct change in Suzana's pedagogical documentation that is relevant to the part played by music. The example curriculum book for 2010 starts with children experimenting with listening to different sounds, with an emphasis on participation and well-being. Kylie had introduced music appreciation into the music activities she shared with children and classical music was an interest she wanted to encourage. Suzana had picked this up and the first page of the scrap book contained observations of the children's response to Vivaldi's *Spring Symphony* and their different approaches to how to express the music visually. Figure 6.1 displays the first-page spread of the 2010 scrap book from September: we can see the references to Vivaldi's *Spring Symphony*, a comment on the teacher-led experience with the river of silk, as well as a recurring theme of using a key image to open different experiences. Children's comments about their pictorial impressions of the sound, referred to by Suzana as cross modal representations, have been included.

This change in the connection between the music programme and happenings in the room supports the differences we have been able to observe over time. Observations recorded in this book reflect the changing status of the formal sessions as the music in Suzana's room gradually melded with the music of the music studio.

FIGURE 6.1 Page of curriculum book

Shared experiences

By the time the third musician started working in the centre, Suzana had already become involved in the music programme, initially through the teachers' singing group, where she said she had been able to connect with staff 'at a different level'. That initiative had improved 'engagement with the specialist music programme' (interview, 14 June 2008). She felt she had always been an active participant in the music sessions in the gallery, and was able to contribute to the music specialist's documentation in order to extend the musical learning into home-room activities. The role of the specialist was beginning to be inclusive of the classroom teachers. Leah had been aware of her feeling of isolation, which had begun to break down with the staff singing group. Later, she would take on more of a 'musician in residence' role, starting to visit the rooms with songs, instruments and musical stories. This occurred while Kylie was also conducting formal music sessions in the gallery, so for a few months the centre had a very strong music programme, strongly supported by staff and parents.

The following observation, taken from the notes of the researcher, describes a visit by Leah to Suzana's room:

> A music lesson today was held in children's playrooms. Suzana and her group were waiting for the music teacher when I arrived at the room. I was interested to see what material Leah would present to the children in the home-room setting.
>
> The session started with a 'getting to know you' name song, aided by a friendly frog puppet. This was followed by a short discussion on what the children had been exploring with Suzana in recent days. This discussion was encouraged by Suzana, who invited the children to describe their experiences and knowledge of the 'sky'. The sky was a theme that was currently a focus in the centre. Leah listened to the children, looked at their drawings and paintings and commented that they had been engaged in some 'beautiful work'.
>
> After continuing with a vocal warm-up and a new welcome song that included movement and body percussion, Leah introduced the idea of beat

by asking the children to try and locate their own heartbeats on different pulse points of the body. One of the children shared that her heartbeat was very fast the other day when she got a present in the mail and became excited when she was opening it. Suzana commented that that is exactly what happens to her heartbeat when she dances. Other children confirmed this as the session proceeded with some Gipsy Balkan music with a strong beat that the children danced too. The children were encouraged to listen for the heartbeat of the music and mark it with different body actions. They took turns to make up movements that we could copy. Suzana swayed like a belly-dancer, which made the children giggle as they tried to imitate this movement.

The session finished with the teacher singing 'Moon Dreaming', a song that followed a journey of a frog's night-time wandering with the moon. The children listened and were able to recall what happened at the end of the frog's journey. Suzana wondered aloud: 'Hm ... I wonder where you would go on a journey?' She suggested she would talk about this later in the afternoon.

Interpretive comment

The session in the children's home-room was a predictable music session on the whole, with a couple of significant differences – the main one being that Suzana had more agency and input in her own space. The session started with an acknowledgement Leah was a visitor and, therefore, a getting to know you song was introduced. Leah then connected to the room by asking what the children had been doing. The space contained memory prompts to assist the discussion and Suzana was able to be an active player by prompting the direction of the discussion. Leah was also able to see the children's art works. The music session then resumed with a welcome song, body percussion and an emerging aim of an exploration of beat. Suzana was more prominent in the movement section. The session finished on a whimsical note that Suzana said she would follow up on later.

> There was a meeting occurring in this session that was a sharing of experience. Leah conducted a music group with the children as a visitor within the room. Taking on the role of the visitor, conducting a familiar type of session in the children's space and acknowledging the activities that occurred in that space made this a bridging activity that had potential to see how, and in what ways, the children could generalise their musical knowledge from one context to another.

The above observation is an indication of how Suzana recorded and shared her work with the children and engaged with staff and parents in the centre community to enhance their work as well. She received resources from others and actively developed their potential. She also discussed her observations, ideas and plans. Suzana used various vehicles for sharing and researching her teaching practice. As well as active engagement and her written curriculum documentation, she kept a special notice board for parents in her room, a journal notebook used with the children during discussions and reflection. Children's thoughts were recorded and often followed through as provocations, as well as being used in her pedagogical documentation. Suzana also became involved in sharing the music of the centre at conferences. During the time the researchers were observing the programme, she twice attended an international performing arts conference and presented a paper. Examples of this sharing include a CD from Kylie, books and pictures to follow the interest in *The Magic Flute*, using the centre notice board and the in-room notice board, her journal notebook, singing and presenting at staff meetings, as well as her conference presentations.

Suzana supported Kylie's attempts to share resources across spaces by preparing a recording of the songs she was introducing to the children. Copies were given to all the centre staff. The CD contained Kylie singing the songs she was exploring with the children, as well as the music they were listening to, movement pieces and some recordings of orchestras and different types of musicians and instruments, all classical. Suzana used the CD that Kylie had recorded for the children and teachers. Kylie reported that most of the generalist staff had used the songs to help the children learn to sing them, but most had not played the CD that contained the music appreciation content or the movement music. Suzana had introduced both CDs to the children and gave equal time to the latter CD and the song CD.

Suzana kept records on the children's learning in a variety of ways. She had notebooks where she would record spontaneous comments and responses by the children to events across the day. Her notes show children's impressions, thoughts and questions in great detail, and she included comments on how she might utilise their interests and ideas to inform her planning. She would also take notes in this book when she was having a group discussion on the mat with the children. They were accustomed to her notebook and would often ask her what she was writing. During the *Magic Flute* project, notes included such comments as: 'The children are beginning to make faces – just like characters in the opera'; and 'they described colours – giving them an emotional character; I am amazed with their memory/ recall of the costumes'. On another occasion L, one of four children, went with the other groups to perform 'The River of Life' for people who attended an inclusive programme that catered for participants with diverse abilities, at the nearby children's farm. Suzana recorded his comments on how different 'that' performance was to the performances at the centre. Another time she wrote that 'he (L) has been singing in his "low voice", just like Sarastro from *The Magic Flute*'. She noted that 'J has found her very high voice; she raises her hand to show she is singing high and says, "My voice is so, soooo high!"' Some of these snippets appeared later in the curriculum book, especially if Suzana had been able to use the children's ideas with the whole group or extend an individual child's interest.

Other forms of documentation that played an important role in the centre were the notice boards. These were significant strategies for establishing a dialogue with the parents about children's learning and development, the educator's knowledge of children's learning and development and the daily activities of the centre. Suzana contributed to the main notice board in the corridor using examples of children's work and thoughts. The information displayed on these boards tended to reflect the project the centre was currently focusing on; each of the specialist teachers would post a weekly plan and accompanying report. Art works from the children were carefully and aesthetically displayed in this space, as described in Chapter 2. Suzana also kept a board in her room especially designed for the parents. This was a panel of approximately 160cm by 50cm providing elaborate visual illustrations, often in miniature, of the children, their activities and their social life within this space. These displays were a means of starting communication with families and arousing the parents' awareness of what children were interested in generally. Such communication assists in building understanding and partnerships with parents, as the panel was designed to introduce 'parents to a quality of knowing that tangibly changes their expectations' (Edwards, Gandini and Forman, 1998, p. 64). The parents also contributed to the value of the parent notice board by commenting on the content and providing extra information about their own child.

Another method Suzana had of sharing musical experiences with staff, children and the wider community was through singing at the centre and presenting at early childhood music conferences. The song 'Eucalypts of Melbourne' (Chapter 7) was composed by Suzana and the children in her room during the United Nations Year of the Forest. Suzana explained that she used the children's familiarity with the surrounding trees and the Yarra river, which was a venue for frequent excursions. Branches of eucalypts were collected and an installation was erected in the children's room at the centre. This installation was used as a stimulus; children were encouraged to think of descriptive words and phrases to explain their own view of the eucalypts and their relationship to these trees. Suzana said the group worked on the poem line by line and, once finished, she felt it made the 'music happen' (informal interview). This description of process helps to explain how the words are the drivers in this particular creation.

Another song, very different musically, became a favourite of all the groups of children –'Sitting in the Sand'. Suzana set a known poem to music and the children had an input into the final version. 'Sitting in the Sand' is by Karla Kuskin and was published in the book of poems *The Sky is Full of Song* in 1983 (Hopkins, 1983). Suzana often recited it to the children. She said: 'I realised a while ago that the poem has got a kind of meditative movement, so I "composed" the existing tune keeping in mind that I wanted the song to reflect serene time at the seaside.'

> Sitting in the sand and the sea comes up
> And you put your hands together
> And you hold them like a cup.
> And you dip them in the ocean* with a swooping kind of motion –
> And before the sea goes out again –
> You have a sip of ocean.

*Suzana swapped original word, water, for ocean

They devised a game: the children would find something in their hand 'before the sea goes out again'. However, the children gave it a different twist by breaking the softness of it at the end by their verbalisations of what they 'found' in their sip of ocean. They became very adventurous in their 'findings' and the singular sea things multiplied and turned into their personal narratives (I found a garden where the mermaids play, three sharks having a battle with a swordfish, a lost crab who was looking for a new home, corals made out of seaweed ice cream …). The song was used for focusing the group before discussion or reflection time, as Suzana called it, and she said it gave everyone a chance to break the silence and say something personal. Since each child offered his/her original narrative, the group could stay focused and listen with interest. Special friends often found the same, or similar, things in their sip of ocean. Suzana said the use of the song was to start by centring children in the warm sand, 'shhhshhh', with sound being added before the singing started, to add to the mood and take the children on a memory, or dreamlike, trip to the ocean, where anything might be possible. This narrative and imaginative use of words and music became popular across the centre.

Another aspect of Suzana's sharing of her music and work with children was the attendance and participation in professional development sessions and education conferences. In 2013 she attended the Early Childhood of the Performing Arts (ECCPA) organised by the Victorian Orff Schulwerk Association (VOSA). The conference was themed 'Learning through Musical Play'. Suzana presented a paper called 'Songlines of the Yarra', which reflected the many musical explorations that the children had enjoyed during trips to the river near the centre. The term 'songlines' is a reference to Aboriginal creation stories and to how the creators' journeys, known as dreaming tracks, across the land and sky could be traced through song. Suzana was introduced to aspects of Aboriginal culture from a project called 'Coming Closer', which involved a children's art exhibition that shared understandings of Aboriginal culture between Australian Aboriginal children and non-indigenous Australian children. Suzana was attracted to the idea of the 'owners of the dreaming' singing the songs of their ancestors to trace their way across the land. This conference paper combined knowledge from the 'Coming Closer' project with the children's familiarity of the Yarra and their sense of space. She presented a paper illustrated by a short DVD and sang for the audience. In the programme for the conference, Suzana said that through the DVD participants would 'be able to see a short film (eight minutes) produced by the teachers, children and a parent, and reflect on the ways the children communicate concepts and aesthetics of their beloved physical space'.

Through these activities of working, documenting, interpreting and presenting findings, Suzana would be considered an example of a teacher researcher. Practitioner research has received increased attention in recent years, especially as early childhood education has become a more serious project for many governments around the world. To have a practitioner researcher with such a commitment to art, music and nature was a valuable addition to the specialist programmes that the ELC provided.

Teacher as researcher

There is a growing conviction in education circles that a focus on pedagogical enquiry by teachers themselves has the potential to improve our knowledge of children's learning and to enhance efforts to improve educational practice. One aspect of the teacher as researcher model is that the children and families involved are more likely to benefit from the findings as the direct connection between the teacher and the research has the capacity to blur the boundaries between research and practice. Simocini, Lasen and Rocco (2014) describe the role of professional development as becoming more constructivist in orientation as there is a growing awareness that the process of teacher learning and knowledge acquisition is something that is active, occurs over time and becomes more layered and complex as it builds on previous experience, content knowledge and pedagogical learning. There is an emphasis on lifelong learning and reflective practice. Being in a centre that has been influenced strongly by the Reggio Emilia early childhood education approaches and notions of emergent curriculum, Suzana was in a context where her interests and skills could be welcomed. Even the story that has unfolded here is an example of something growing over time. Suzana was in the centre for the time of two of the specialist musicians described here and, across the incumbency of the two, her own connectedness to the music programme changed dramatically.

In 2009, Australia introduced, for the first time, an early childhood national curriculum and proponents suggest it offers new ways of thinking and theorising about children, especially with the attention afforded the idea of pedagogical documentation in the framework. For many years, practitioners and researchers attracted to the Reggio Emilia approach have considered documentation a source of reflection, communication, transparency and even a guide to progressive action. In Suzana, we present an example of a teacher who, through her own pedagogical documentation, can share her journey with these children as they explore aspects of the music in their lives.

Pedagogical documentation is a tool where data is recorded and meaning created. The meanings that Suzana has given in her actions and records on children's understandings and explorations in music have been investigative and collaborative. She was able to track the processes of the children she was working with, plus her own longer journey across the two musicians.

From these illustrations of Suzana, the music in the centre (both the specialist programme and Suzana's contribution) and the role of the children we can get a picture of the children's competence when exposed to sophisticated and meaningful experiences. Some were serendipitous and the shining moment was improved upon, some were carefully planned, while some grew through the relationships, interest and knowledge that developed around particular themes. All of these were recorded by Suzana.

Conclusion: intentional teaching

Suzana's approach to her planning, recording, interpretations and the development of relational pedagogies all reflect the influence of the notion of an 'intentional teacher'. Although she is reluctant to specifically label herself as an intentional teacher, Suzana recognises that she incorporated intentional teaching into her approach at this time. The new Australian early childhood curriculum has taken the notion of intentional teaching from the High Scope curriculum (Epstein, 2005), which is based on the three elements of interactions, the learning environment and the 'plan-do-review' approach to teaching. Suzana uses planning time in a creative manner. She would have frequent group and small group meetings with the children and the planning, doing, reviewing activities were rolled into a seamless process. Bouncing off the children's previous experiences, she encouraged planning and problem-solving through her provocations. Examples of provocations mentioned in this chapter include the postcard of Mozart and the computer, as well as children's own questions being put back to the group, as in, 'How do you make a bear look like a butterfly?' This allowed the children to revisit experiences and their own perceptions and ideas about those experiences, and they were given the opportunity to pool their efforts in group activities like songwriting 'The Eucalypts of Melbourne' and composing 'Sitting in the Sand'.

The learning environment and the type of aesthetics Suzana enjoyed and used are reflected in the page of the curriculum book presented in Figure 6.1. Miniatures (reminiscent of Montessori), an eclectic use of colour and commercial and hand-drawn visuals create a busy impression, full of messages that need to be carefully studied. Many displays are seen around the room, such as a table for special objects, a branch from the trees by the river and the special notice board for parents. The room was divided into small spaces delineated by chairs, cushions and rugs. The space for the group discussion was situated in the middle of the room, surrounded by all the smaller areas and, therefore, full of visual stimuli and memories.

Suzana assessed the children's learning, and her own, through pedagogical documentation. This was a powerful tool in her hands. She was an effective communicator who could tell the stories of the learning, the explorations, experiments and happenings in the room. Her enthusiasm made her interactions with the children vibrant and exciting, and her love of the music made the atmosphere exciting.

In this chapter we have given a brief view of how a generalist teacher can bring her own skills and interest to the music programme. She was not only a support to the music specialist, but also brought her own training and knowledge of music, her background in European folk music and her confidence to engage in composition and forms of musical activity not often undertaken in a pre-school. The last music leader we refer to in this book (Chapters 7 and 8) is one of the generalist teachers in the centre. Rei possesses formal music skills, enormous enthusiasm and has stepped forward as a music leader as the third musician, Kylie, has moved overseas to pursue other interests. This circumstance is becoming less unusual in early childhood education centres; research is emerging of teachers becoming *de facto* music teachers, as the arts, especially music, are suffering because of an imbalance in the curriculum that sees even early childhood curriculum focusing on literacy and numeracy skills to the detriment of richer learning. Suzana is a bridge between the work of the music specialist in the gallery and the general trained teacher becoming a centre music leader.

7

THE EARLY LEARNING CENTRE CHOIR

Introduction and background

This chapter is about an ELC choir that brought together children, teachers and researchers on a unusual journey of discovery for a pre-school. The voices of the children as they engaged in the singing project were expressed through pedagogical documentation, children's drawings and through the 'choir' of combined voices of children and teachers. One of the author/researchers of this book became the main conductor of the choir. This was a position the children assumed the researcher would undertake. She had been a participant observer in earlier projects and the children turned to her as a participant when choir practices started. Discussion with the musician, director and the researcher meant that the children's role in choosing the researcher as a main protagonist was respected. The musician, director and other educators also played lead roles in the choir and its performances, leading to a change in relationships between the specialist music programme and the generalist teachers.

The notion of 178 pre-school children and fifteen teachers singing together may surprise some. This ELC, however, has had a tradition of children and teachers performing and the founding of the choir came about naturally in this context, as the children had previous experience in singing as a whole group (Chapter 3), as well as performing at end of term concerts and being exposed to performances (Chapter 4). The children were the protagonists in this initiative by originally introducing choir into their dramatic play. The children's choir evolved from the teachers' singing group at the centre, which had become a catalyst that inspired the children's dramatic play of setting up choirs and conducting and singing for each other during spontaneous play. This chapter describes how this musical experience unfolded and how the choir became an integral part of the centre's culture. We present documentation on the children's choir, adult roles and participation, as well as providing a background. 'Performance' is one notion often missing in early childhood arts and this is an aspect of music in this centre that has been developed as a visible part of the curriculum. The children's understanding of performance grew as they played and also experienced formal rehearsals, and the different roles that a performance consists of, including audience, performer, conductor, instrumentalist, reporter, even illustrator.

A staff singing group had been established previously (Chapter 4) with the joint aims of integrating the specialist music programme into the music initiatives that were occurring in the separate groups within the centre and bringing staff together through singing, the latter being a particular hope of the musician Leah's. Group feelings, culture, relationships, collaborative action and accomplishment were the phenomena being explored. The teachers' singing group project was designed to culminate in a performance by the teachers for the children. This performance raised strong emotions from the staff, who recorded their experiences and feelings in interviews after the concert. The children also reacted strongly to the teachers' sharing of their music experience through the performance. The children were aware of the role of 'audience'; they are often involved in activities where the teachers take the lead, or plan provocations (Chapter 6). At times the educators' roles are clearly instructional and children listen to the educators presenting stories, poetry and models, as well as the reading of stories and scaffolding initiatives.

> At the performance, the children were taken aback – this was unusual behaviour – our teachers don't usually do this, so why are they doing it? They may not have understood the idea of teachers as performers, and that role change caused some confusion for them. A couple of children seemed a little embarrassed – part of not understanding that teachers would do this … They were genuinely engaged – there was a deep level of engagement. They were interested in the change and were trying to process this. They generally enjoyed it and, as we did it on other occasions, there was strong acceptance of this. And they were respectful – they understood the protocol, gave everyone a clap. (Interview, Director, 19 May 2010)

The unexpected consequences of the teachers singing for the children had implications for future musical activity, with the development of what was called the ELC Choir.

The ELC Choir

One day, the educators noticed that a small group of children had arranged themselves into a 'choir' and were performing some songs for their peers, who applauded enthusiastically. On further observation, the adults realised that the performance of the children had been inspired by the teachers' singing group that had practised and performed the previous term. The children were acting out a performance, standing in a straight line, with a child conducting vigorously at the front. This event took place on a veranda with an elevated stage that made it a perfect amphitheatre for the occasion. Later on, this same group of children was invited to sing at the centre's weekly assembly. Their performance was received with enthusiasm by the child audience and the choir project began.

On the day of their first 'official' performance, at the weekly assembly, the group of children confidently presented the lullaby '*Inanay*' that they had enjoyed listening to from the CD of *The Choir of Hard Knocks* (2007). *The Choir of Hard Knocks* was initiated by Jonathon Welch as a community singing project with homeless and disadvantaged people. The choir and the CD caught the public imagination in Australia. '*Inanay*' is a popular Australian Aboriginal song which has been a favourite with pre-school teachers for many years. The children's response to the song on the CD may have been the result of already being familiar with the song; they were pleased that they had knowledge of an artefact that received a lot of public adult attention.

All children in the centre, their teachers, two music specialists, researchers and the centre director were involved in the choir. The music specialists, the centre director and one of the researchers took responsibility for collaborative planning and for identifying the overarching purpose for this specialised musical programme. It was thought the concept of the choir performance, as a collective aesthetic communication, would allow for collaborative learning coloured by the powerful feelings and emotions that singing can generate. Engagement with challenging new musical activities included choir behaviours (breathing, posture), singing in unison, conducting, choreographing a performance and responding to musical accompaniment. As was the case with the adults' singing group, a decision was made to record the choir events from the beginning as one of the research projects being carried out in the centre. To fulfil the research component of the project it was decided that each session would be videotaped to enable the planning team to evaluate the children's responses to proposed activities and to provide an opportunity for children to view their own performances throughout the course of the programme. Such revisiting and critiquing of events adds a valuable dimension to children's interpretation experience.

Through their music sessions and the centre's traditional end of year concerts, the children were already familiar with the concept of performing; being in a choir aimed to add another level of understanding and, in turn, presented the children with new expectations. Rehearsals typically began with a playful voice warm-up, where children were led through a series of vocal exercises designed to draw attention to the use of the voice, breathing and posture. These rehearsals also included opportunities for singing known songs and, very soon, a repertoire emerged that connected children to their interests and their group learning programmes.

The children's eagerness to sing in a choir was investigated when the researcher/conductor decided to explore the notion of 'choir' and choirs around the world with the children. A presentation featuring a wide range of photographs and YouTube videos of choirs were shown to the children via a projector in the music space in the gallery. The following journal entry gives an idea of the children's ideas and interest.

Excerpt from researcher/conductor's journal

Context

Introductory session at the beginning of the term one, including new children at the ELC Choir. Location was the music studio and participants were the Wednesday groups, consisting of 86 children and thirteen teachers.

> Last week, I introduced a concept of a conductor to the children. We viewed a presentation with different recordings, via projector. The children and the teachers had an opportunity to see a number of conductors in action. We explored a variety of compositions, featuring different facial and hand expressions. The children were observant and made comments about the music, qualifying it as 'strong', 'quiet', 'sad', 'happy', 'fast', 'scary', 'funny', 'curious', 'complicated', 'film music', 'music for singing', 'music for dancing' and 'sleep music'. We talked about music terms, such as dynamics (*piano* and *forte*) and revisited some tempos – andante, moderato, presto and allegro. The children were already familiar with these words from their music sessions and liked the Italian language. We agreed to check if we all remembered the words next time. Today, we revisited the role of a conductor. This time, the presentation contained photographs of eminent conductors in concerts. As soon as the slides started, the children started shouting out their impressions of the conductors in the photographs: 'firm', 'gentle', 'cross', 'fast', 'be quiet', 'loud', 'pretty hair' (for a woman), 'slow down', 'wait', 'hurry', 'curious', 'watch!', 'go', 'confused'.
>
> The children intently studied YouTube videos, in the presentation, of Aboriginal, Australian and African children's choirs performing, absorbing and observing a number of relevant aspects of these children's actions; the ELC children commented that the children in the YouTube choirs stand still; do not bump into each other, as this would make an argument instead of singing; listen to each other's voices; they open wide their mouths; watch the conductor; remember the words; they sometimes clap their hands; sometimes there are instruments; sometimes they are all girls, or all boys; sometimes they sing high and low and sometimes medium; they wear the same beautiful colours.
>
> The children were interested in conducting and remarked that I was their conductor, as I told them what song and how to sing and had a stick to make sure they see better and follow. One of the girls added that Anna (four-year-old friend from Eucalypt room) conducted them outside, too, and that I should add her picture to the slides. We concluded the session with playing a conducting game where the children followed my stick and sang high, low, fast and slow, accordingly. Conducting became a popular 'act', and many children took turns at it.

Conducting was one of the languages of music that captured the children's imaginations. Conducting is a musical expression that unifies a group through the reading of visible gestures. As noted in this observation, these gestures interpret the music by instructing the performers on such musical elements as tempo, duration, dynamics, rhythm, beat and colour. This is a highly individualised activity that is very public. The conductor must overtly instruct the singers and is being creative by interpreting the meaning of the song. The interpretation is communicated through meaningful musical elements. One child, A, liked to play the part of conductor when the children 'played' choirs. The children stood on a log to keep in a line so they could be a choir; then A would pick up a stick and become a conductor. Although she was on the ground and, therefore, physically lower than the choir, she became a powerful figure because of the role she had adopted. Watching a recording of the children's play, we could see that her hand movements were indicative of her understanding of the mood of the song and she clearly remembered the conducting models presented previously. Through this introduction to choirs and choir activities, such as the conducting, the children gained much insight into the discipline needed to produce a collaborative performance. This made them more appreciative of the role of rehearsal.

Rehearsals

Given the number of children participating in this enterprise, groupings were established and children happily joined together, comfortable with each other within the space. The children would arrive in their home-room groups of Wattles, Blue Gums, Banksias, Eucalypts and Waratahs. The children sat in their groups with their teachers, but not always in the same part of the music studio.

As the idea of performance became more dominant, masking tape was used to encourage standing in straight lines or to mark a spot for a solo or instrumental piece, by an individual, or a small group. Therefore, rehearsals often contained whole-group singing, percussion instruments and solo performances. Very early, it became evident that the performance element of the experience was of significance and opportunities to perform were offered. Children performed in small and large groups for each other; there were children who sang solos and duets and teachers performed solos, duets and in small groups.

The rehearsals were segmented into different parts. Usually, they would begin with the centre director reading poetry. The children were familiar with this and were familiar with the content of the particular book she read from. Occasionally, the poems would be put to music and became a part of the repertoire – for example, 'Hurt No Living Thing' by Christina Rossetti. Sometimes, the children would comment and/or recite with the director; sometimes the poem/s were closely related to the choir repertoire or a significant event that had just occurred or was being discussed at the centre. After these introductory activities, the choir part of the rehearsal would officially start with a vocal warm-up. Initially, these vocal exercises were offered by the conductor/researcher. Traditional choir warm-ups like the breathing exercise '1,121,12321,1234321 etc.', sung on consecutive scale notes (e.g., on 'C, CDC, CDEDC, CDEFEDC etc.), were taught to the children.

Once the children became more familiar with the concept and purpose of preparing vocal chords to sing, some came up with their own ideas and were often invited to lead the warm-up. For instance, one of the children proposed that one side of the room sing a made-up chant 'Leggo-Peggo' and the other would respond, 'Peggo-Leggo'. His friend suggested the groups swap and repeat the 'Leggo-Peggo' exercise. Other children joined in this activity of designing their own material. One teacher's notes reflect this trend:

> This morning, Hazel came in with a present for her friends: a poem she had created on a piece of paper as soon as she got out of bed. She had used an A4 page and a stamp, and placed the word PERFECTION in numerous directions. She read it out: 'perfection, perfection, perfection, perfection'. Her friends looked a little surprised and one of them suggested that this could not be a poem as it only had one word. So, I decided to read the word 'perfection' in different ways changing its tone, character, accent, articulation, dynamics and volume. This made the children realise that now it sounded like a poem and one of the boys proposed we sing it. Hazel grabbed the paper and sang: 'perfection, perfection, perfection, perfection' ascending on each repetition. The rest of the group spontaneously joined in and we continued to experiment with the word, just like in warm-ups in choir. Later in the afternoon, Hazel presented 'Perfection' in our choir rehearsal. (Teacher's notes, 2013)

The repertoire and order of the songs varied from children's to teachers' or researcher's choice. When there was a coming performance, songs were usually practised in the order they would be performed. Singing was a dominant part of the rehearsals and it often involved movement, an opportunity to move around space and sometimes physically interact with others. For example, when singing 'Siyahumba', an African song, the children were invited to march around the room. Some time was also given to discussion and reflection. During a number of sessions, children viewed their performances, via projected video data onto a blank wall, and it was clear that they learned a great deal from being given the opportunity to critically reflect on their participation.

The idea of revisiting the rehearsals so children could explore and rediscover their learning in a context of joint musical activity comes from the concept of documentation associated with Reggio Emilia. Pedagogical documentation is used by educators to record activities, to help make children's ideas visible, to develop their own theories to share with others and to influence future learning. Through this process, the children and adults enter a cycle of co-construction of knowledge. The recordings of the rehearsals with the children were available for continuous investigation which, hopefully, meant some of the projects might have a more extensive life as children in the future might choose to explore the 'lessons' previous children in the centre have left for them. The children engaged with the videos by recognising the familiar and commenting on what was different, like particular children not being present, their outfits and sometimes joining in the music. Gradually, their comments took account of more detail and they even made comparative comments about the recording being viewed and those viewed previously – for example, qualitative comments about a song sounding better when there were more children in the group.

From participating in the rehearsals, the children gained a sense of self and others as they co-constructed meanings about shared musical activity, working together and sometimes achieving a 'togetherness' that was quite euphoric. This synergy was more likely to be observed during rehearsals than actual performances. The choir and the performances assisted the children in consolidating some of the skills and concepts encountered during the music sessions. This brought added knowledge and experience of a formal joint action, the performance, where space and sound were not spontaneous, but the sense of accomplishment when 'it comes together' is an experience that is usually associated with adult pleasure. The elements of self-discipline, self-regulation and practice required were all part of this experience and were more obvious during rehearsals. Another valuable aspect of the choir was the repertoire, which was more sophisticated and diverse than would often be used in an early childhood programme, as this repertoire was required to be varied enough to make an interesting performance. The sheer number of children and adults involved meant that the repertoire had to be negotiated across different groups, ages and preferences.

Repertoire of the choir

During rehearsals the children encountered many different types of music, songs and roles to engage with. The repertoire was diverse and influenced by the musicians. For example, over the period of the research, the children moved from being familiar with songs about the environment to including songs of a more classical nature.

During the choir practice, children were consulted about the repertoire. They were asked which songs they would like to sing and which songs should be included in the concert performances. They were offered a choice of familiar songs and new songs. The unfamiliar songs were introduced in a variety of ways – for example, by a YouTube recording, or by being sung to them accompanied by the guitar or piano. Examples of some of the songs introduced to the children were 'Peter's Song', from the Eurovision Song Contest; 'The River is Flowing', written by one of the musicians; a contemporary Australian song, 'Black Swan'; and a children's favourite, the Canadian 'Canoe Song'. In addition, an original song by a homeroom staff member and the children she worked with, 'The Eucalypts of Melbourne', was composed. This song was initially written to be performed to other children in the centre, but became so popular among the children it became a mainstay for public performances.

In this section on repertoire, we have decided to unpack two of the songs the children were enthusiastic about. These two songs have very different providences and illustrate the diversity of the material that the children engaged with. They are examples of the value of mixing familiarity, imagination and complexity. The first song is the original song written by a staff member and children, 'The Eucalypts Song' (which the children called 'The Eucalypts of Melbourne'), the second is the Canadian canon, the 'Canoe Song'. 'The Eucalypts of Melbourne', because it is an original piece, we discuss as an historical artefact of the centre. We briefly analyse its musical properties, as an example of meaning being the dominant element that has been expressed through a complex form. This is not a typical song for children, but it was understood and popular with the children because of their strong feeling of connectedness to the words, and the music itself has been crafted to the words. We recount the history of the writing of the song, describe its musical elements and comment on how these define the verbal sentiments.

The second song, 'Canoe Song', is illustrated as a learning story that was documented from the end of year performance. Learning stories (Carr, 2001) are narratives used as assessment tools to gauge children's learning and make what learning is taking place visible. They are a common observation tool used in early childhood programmes in New Zealand, Australia and the UK. Learning stories are based on an exploration of children's learning dispositions and record their active participation and levels of engagement in particular activities. They are a sociocultural method of describing and explicating meaning from events. Learning stories are popular internationally in early childhood education for assessment and research and have been used to analyse young children's musical experiences (Acker and Nyland, 2012). We use learning stories more extensively in Chapter 8. In this first example, we describe the song, 'The Eucalypt Tree'.

'The Eucalypt Tree'

Using the children's knowledge and interests, the Eucalypt group's teacher decided to encourage a collaborative activity of composition. It was decided the song would be about the nearby river and would reflect the stories the Eucalypt group children had told each other as they visited the river. Using the familiar and introducing prosodic elements of repetition and chorus to give a pattern to the song, the teacher and the children produced 'The Eucalypt Tree'.

'The Eucalypt Tree' is a cheerful and short piece with vivid and colourful imagery. The localised subject was partially created and suggested by the children, which makes it easier and suitable for them to remember and helps explain their enthusiasm.

Melodically, it lies within the reach of most adult voices – the general *tessitura* is about the interval of a fifth, and the lowest note is an octave below the highest. The melodic line moves by stepped motion, sometimes by a third. The octave leap draws attention, but it is always predictable, as can be noticed in the 'Canoe Song', where the children were able to predict when the octave jump was coming and, in that case, substituted a pitch change with a dynamic that had the same dramatic effect. Both verse and chorus of 'The Eucalypt Tree' consist of small catchy motivic cells, which the children repeated enthusiastically and often.

FIGURE 7.1 'The Eucalypt Tree'

The characteristic rhythmic element of this piece is its irregularity. There are down-beats that feel like up-beats and the constant change of metre in the chorus makes this an interesting piece of music. The word flow has a speech-like pattern that is not broken up by common time rests or breaks, which would privilege the basic beat over the meaning of the words. The Eucalypt children liked this song, which captivated their feelings for surrounding nature and the city they live in. They shared it with others at choir rehearsals and, since everyone responded to it so readily, the song was included in the end of year concert. It was not an easy song for young children, but one that came from familiar knowledge and strong interest and now has a life of its own in this centre. The next example is presented very differently. This is a song that is commonly sung with young children and would be frequently heard in pre-school and school settings. As it would be considered part of a usual repertoire, we have chosen the learning story format to describe the children's involvement with this song.

'Canoe Song': a learning story

'Canoe Song': performance observation

Context

This was the end of year performance and it was held in the assembly hall of a local secondary college. The setting was a formal stage area and theatre seats for the audience. All five groups from the centre presented a dance to start the concert. Staying in their dance-costumes, the children lined up, three-deep, across the stage for the singing section of the concert. Masking tape on the floor was used to enable the children to find their positions. Masking tape was a strategy used by musicians in the weekly music sessions when they wanted the children in a particular formation. The researcher/conductor adopted the practice for the choir because of the number of children involved.

> **'Canoe Song' (Canadian folk song)**
> Our paddle's keen and bright,
> Flashing like silver;
> Swift as the wild goose flight,
> Dip, dip and swing.
> Dip, dip and swing them back,
> Flashing like silver;
> Swift as the wild goose flight,
> Dip, dip and swing.

The children sang this song in three groups. All groups started by singing 'Dip, dip and swing'; and the older children continued to sing 'Dip, dip and swing' as an ostinato throughout, with one of the home-room teachers conducting. Conductors for the other two groups were the musician and another home-room teacher. They were slightly out of time. As the song got going, the ostinato group held their part well; the middle group, when they got to signature pitch rise 'silver', shouted the last syllable instead of attempting the pitch rise. The group at the end sang more softly and the musician could be heard singing above them. From the video recording, all children were participating. There were different levels of participation, with one of the older children gazing steadfastly ahead, with his lips moving slightly, while another child bowed so enthusiastically at the applause, she almost fell forward and had to push herself up off the floor.

The learning dispositions associated with the learning story are: taking an interest; being involved; persisting with difficulty; expressing an idea or a feeling; and taking responsibility. These are accompanied by a short-term review and a comment on how the learning dispositions that were visible might be encouraged to appear in more complex ways or across contexts. The learning story was designed to be used for individual children, groups and a whole programme. In this instance, all children in the programme were involved.

Taking an interest

These children were taking an interest in that they were all participating in a joint activity; they were presenting familiar material in an unfamiliar context and were coping very well.

Being involved

Involvement was evident across the group as no child stood out as not participating. They were able to pay attention for a sustained period of time.

Persisting with difficulty

This was a difficult task for pre-schoolers. The song has a pitch range that was not comfortable for at least one group and they solved this problem by enthusiastically shouting when they got to the high note. Such a large number singing a round is a challenge and, not surprisingly, the timing factor was influenced by the fact they were standing in lines across the stage and, therefore, each child could not see most of the other children, or hear clearly. Adding an ostinato to the round made the sound extremely complex. The children showed no hesitation, faced with these challenges, and sang through to the end.

Expressing an idea or feeling

As this was a rehearsed piece, this disposition was not so easy to observe. The individual children's comments upon the story did indicate different approaches to the experience of performance. One was engaged, but not confident to perform and, therefore, was seen intently watching the adult in front and mouthing the words. The child who did an exaggerated bow was fully in the space of a performance and she was a performer.

Taking responsibility

This could be observed through the contribution made by each child. All were observed to participate, albeit at different levels. There was a concerted effort until the end and they remained in place and disciplined as they waited for the next song.

Short-term review

This performance was an indication of how a group of young children, with preparation and appropriate experiences, can display self-discipline and be able to participate in a very large group without discomfort. There were varying levels of innovation in how they dealt with the difficulties of the context and the music itself.

What next?

What emerged from this observation was that the children were able to work together as a large group. The singing and the round were difficult and these music issues could be pursued in a more playful context. Deconstructing known songs, making up and playing with their own ostinato patterns, playing pitch games with their bodies and voices and experimenting with rounds and companion songs could help them become more familiar with some of the musical activities that were involved in this particular song. This would mean breaking the experience down and single concepts being practised and played with across contexts.

Performances

In the introduction, we mentioned the different musical roles that the children experienced. During rehearsals and performances the children gained various skills as members of the choir and their conceptual knowledge of music as a language and an art form grew. For example, a number of children who enjoyed the choir have continued to be formally associated with singing groups and contact the centre to share stories of their activities. The children have gained an awareness of performance participation, and of being an audience. The children were more relaxed and spontaneous during rehearsals than during formal performances, suggesting an awareness of audience. This would have a strong impact on some for future learning situations. The children, as audience, were able to focus on other children and teachers performing in a way that expressed their deep appreciation for the choir.

Another discussion of children as audience has been an exploration of the child's role and the potential learning that occurs when the children are the audience (Schiller, 2005). The child as audience is becoming a focus of other areas of the arts. For example, the visual arts programmes, observed in Reggio Emilia, have a strong emphasis on children as active interpreters of the works of others (e.g., Savva and Trimis, 2005). The ELC uses the music studio as a special gallery for children's art work (Chapter 2). Therefore, the children are always being reminded of their work and the work of others when they are in the music space. During the choir, the teachers explored the role of performer and the audience as a means of helping the children gain an understanding of shared space, to interpret curriculum, to critically interact and to build relationships.

The notion of performance is a theme that runs throughout this chapter. The idea of young children as performers is often overlooked in the early childhood arts literature and there are those who would not espouse such activity as it is too far removed from spontaneous play, a favoured medium for learning in early childhood. In the ELC, performance has a unique space where children can celebrate their knowing and vicariously experience strong emotions in a safe environment. Traditionally, children are expected to sing in pre-schools, schools and community spaces and often the activity is not theorised. The choir has been a research project since its inception and below we give two observations of performance, one formal and one an example of an emergent curriculum.

Formal performance

The first formal public performance was outside, under the centre's veranda, and saw 187 children coming together to 'Sing for the Earth' for a large group of family and friends. At this time, the children shared their song repertoire, featuring: '*Inanay Capuana*', 'The River is Flowing', 'Hurt No Living Thing', 'Celebrate the Rain' and 'Peter's Song'. According to the director and some of the teachers, these songs were specifically chosen to communicate the depth of feeling and respect the children had developed for the earth and its creatures during their projects for the International Year of Earth Sciences.

This collective singing was an exercise in using music to make connections. The children frequently visited the river near the centre, an old convent that had become a community hub and a children's farm. Nature was something actively explored in the programme and the children had developed strong relationships with the particular surrounds. Favourite trees, branches, places to sit and places to observe birds and other creatures were all part of the earth science project, so the children could explore ideas in the abstract and relate them to their own experiences. The performance indicated how seriously the participants took the endeavour. The subject was one the children had shown enduring interest in and continue to do so. Levels of involvement were challenging when so many children shared a stage, but we observed that, in this large group of children, if they could not see the conductor they would reference the timing from each other. There was no sign of obvious distraction. The didactic nature of the songs and the nature message being explored made this an enjoyable experience for the children and was a significant event for all.

Performance as an emergent curriculum

The Blue Gum room children and their teachers went on regular visits to the local river, where they explored different plants and observed some of the inhabitants. An activity that developed spontaneously was the performing of the choir songs by the river bank. At one stage, the teacher and the children investigated sounds of the surrounds, the river, the wind in the trees, the birds, distant traffic. On one of these visits, the Blue Gum teacher and the children recorded their sound-data, decorating a tree by writing or dictating labels, to express the sounds they associated with the tree and the habitat around it. This led them to symbolically explore the sounds they could hear and Figures 7.2–7.4 indicate their understanding of notation, and the connection between sound source and notation. Figure 7.2 displays the child's interest in formal notation and is highly literate; Figure 7.3 is quite an imaginative sound-scape; Figure 7.4 is an interesting combination of representations of the creatures and events that make the sounds, and the music notation to accompany these pictures.

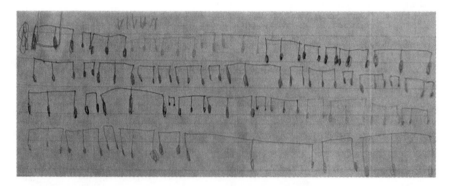

FIGURE 7.2 Child's notation

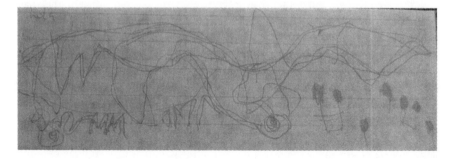

FIGURE 7.3 Child's notation and pictures

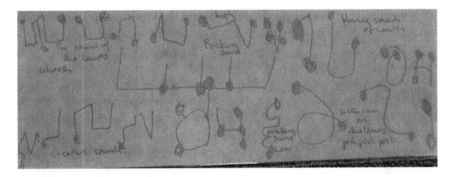

FIGURE 7.4 Notation, pictures and words

This use of the choir songs, the notion of choir, trips to the river, formal and informal knowledge of symbols imaginatively employed by the children are examples of the emergent curriculum that is an important part of the centre's philosophy.

Response of teachers and parents

The ELC teachers have contributed to the choir in many meaningful ways. Through singing, conducting, guiding children in space and activities, documenting and reporting on choir-related experiences, they displayed ownership when things went well and were thoughtful and reflective when things were 'out of tune'. They started to add comments and suggestions when they thought they could usefully share and help solve issues that arose. They gradually started tapping more and more into the choir activities and this led to heightened musical participation. One teacher offered to accompany a song on the piano, another volunteered that she had knowledge of the flute, others were happy to work with children on percussion instruments while others conducted the children in rounds when required. This offering of music knowledge, from the generalist teachers, was a new phenomenon. Only one teacher had previously volunteered to take a proactive role in music activities.

This participation on behalf of the teachers brought the researchers back to one of the discussions that had been ongoing during the research process regarding the role of the expert in an arts-based programme. We had observed there is often a distance between the musician and other artists in the centre and generalist teachers. This distance has taken many forms: lack of familiarity on the part of the musician with the everyday programme, generalist staff feeling shy about 'doing music' when they think the musician might observe or hear them and even an attitude that music is a specialist's field that should be left to the specialists. Therefore, to see generalist teachers come forward to share music skills within the programme was a sign the choir was helping roles to merge. Even during the term the teachers' singing group was practising this did not happen. The singing group was very much directed by the music specialist, though some did make repertoire suggestions.

A number of parents actively participated in the rehearsals and performances. A survey was conducted to ascertain parent perceptions of the choir and the benefits they thought had arisen from the project. The parents thought the development of the choir had generated a number of benefits. They expressed their satisfaction and support of the choir through their participation in rehearsals and performances and via written feedback through the survey. The following are examples of a couple of their comments and indicates the power and effect this musical experience had on their awareness of aspects of music in everyday events, like dramatic play, children's growing musical competence, imagination and ideas associated with the children's choir play. The quotes below are examples of imaginative generalisation, skill and emotional development, self-awareness and confidence, indicating the parents' detailed regard for their children's learning.

> A choir has reinforced T's interest in music and singing. It has given him a sense of singing with a group – how you stand as a choir, singing with others. He has commented on a picture of a group of birds that they are standing like a choir.

> D seems to be able to pick up and remember the lyrics of the songs very quickly, the choir has enhanced this skill. It has also helped her 'range' and she can hit the notes more often. Singing brings out a great sensitivity in her, which is lovely to see.

> Very strong impact. Our daughter wants to continue singing in the choir, has already asked if her new school would have one. When she sings along to her CDs she really notices the emphasis – loud, soft, etc. – and is very aware of the tune.

Summary of emerging themes

The centre has always had a strong arts programme and musicians have been employed for a number of years, but the choir has introduced different elements and potential relationships into the setting which already had commitment to child-centred curriculum and the centrality of expressive activities. The themes that have emerged throughout this chapter include the following:

- The child/children as protagonist/s
- The discipline of a choir – rehearsals, performance, audience
- Complexity of the music (familiar/unfamiliar)
- Parental support
- Relating the choir to philosophy of the centre.

The music was a cultural tool, used to create shared meaning among a specific cultural group within a specific context. We have, therefore, drawn on the performance as the goal of tool-mediated activity (Vygotsky, 1978) to try to explain this enterprise. In her interview, the director reported on being influenced by *The Choir of Hard Knocks* and the fact that, in New Zealand, in early childhood centres, at educators' meetings and at conferences, singing is used in a strongly ritualistic way to develop feelings of connectedness and belonging. The music specialist said her inspiration for the group came from her experience in community singing. She believed singing could bring a feeling of health and well-being and had introduced this idea to the staff.

Teachers' observations and parent feedback provided substantial evidence of individual child skill development. Aspects such as listening, singing in tune, pitch and rhythmic awareness, dynamic expression and diction have been observed to develop over time. As skills have emerged and children have demonstrated their capacities to embrace challenges, the content for investigation has become more complex. In this last part of the chapter, we comment on the emerging themes and discuss unexpected consequences.

The children as protagonists

The children were the protagonists in the choir project on a number of levels. As children, they used the language of play to express what they had become interested in – in this case, aspects of group singing. Through their extensive previous experience in performances, both as performers and audience, they could understand the concept of formal drama and this gave them rich data to work with. The connections across all of the arts in the centre, in relation to the idea of performance, included the *Boorai* gallery, displays in a corridor, the end of year concert, the assemblies, excursions and the staff singing group. This experience and the strength of children's play as an expressive voice provided the underpinning for the enterprise, which demanded high levels of self-discipline and shared discipline.

The discipline of a choir: rehearsals, performance, audience

The children's understanding of the choir was partly formed by their strong interest in adult activity and also by the accessibility of digital media, which made it possible for them to be able to explore aspects of the notion of choir on a conceptual level, as they could revisit events and consolidate ideas through questioning, surmising and discussion. Their comments were insightful, practical, reflective and sometimes innovative in providing a new, or different, lens onto the material presented. They also made some strong general leaps of the imagination by being able to transpose themselves into the world of recorded performers. For example, when some suggested that Anna should be among the images of the conductors in the presentation they were making this jump.

The choir also brought with it the idea of new disciplines that the children had not been familiar with before. The idea of formal practice was new; exploring this idea through YouTube helped the children expropriate and internalise the activities they were being introduced to. Therefore, the children could meet the centre and adults and their performance plans halfway, as they had the advantage of a variety of information at their disposal to aid in their own interpretations of the choir as a collaborative venture.

This was important because not only were these children practising and inventing new skills, they were also beginning to realise the value of the singing, performing, the instrumentation, practising to improve a skill and the gratification that could be experienced when these efforts came together. This brought with it a sense of shared responsibility and meant they welcomed strategies, like masking tape on the floor to guide them.

Complexity of the music

As described, the repertoire was diverse in subject, musical style and complexity, language and origins, and ranged from children's songs to original compositions and songs from different cultures. Figures 7.2–7.4 – featuring children's theories and interpretations of notations, sound and narrative in music – are an example of how the choir enabled, or enhanced, music as a purposeful, expressive activity that could be enacted with skill. The music that was shared, and the enthusiasm displayed by the children, is an indication of their competence when presented with interesting and layered experiences.

Parental support

Most parents were actively supportive of the choir. Support levels differed, but what is evidenced from the quotes included in this chapter is the parents' awareness of the children's growing musical competence. The insights represented in the three quotes reflect awareness of the children's developing world views and different approaches to the choir as a learning experience. We have a display of imagination as a child sees the choir in the line of birds, comments about the child's connecting pitch and lyrics to help her explore meaning and another where the child was concentrating on skill development through practising with CDs. The parents' detailed observations of their children's learning suggest how valuable this enterprise was.

Relating the choir to the philosophy of the centre

The ELC is committed to an emergent curriculum, described in Chapter 2, and the choir is an example of a project that emerged through adult and child joint interests and experiences. Reggio Emilia is one of the exemplars that provided a model on how to celebrate children's competence, voice and rights. This story was an example of project-based curriculum and the principles of the emergent curriculum, as practised in this centre. As discussed in Chapter 2, principles of emergent curriculum include responding to children's interests (the children were the protagonists); activities are self-directed and often open ended and we saw this combination of approaches frequently throughout the choir project. Emergent curriculum depends on initiative and intrinsic motivation and this is probably the component that kept the choir going for parents, staff and children. Co-construction of meaning is an important feature; this could be seen between the children themselves, between children and educators, educators and musicians and, to a lesser extent, parents. The role of the adults was crucial in advancing the events of the choir as it unfolded and one of the roles of adults, when using a creative, open-ended approach to curriculum, was to note children's questions and curiosity and devise ways to extend on them. All of these elements could be observed during this project. In the next chapter, examples of a teacher devising provocations, including using the children's questions and comments, are presented to indicate how children's thinking can be challenging and challenged when working in a satisfying environment.

Unexpected consequences

A consequence of this project was a change in some of the educators' attitudes towards the music and themselves as participants. From the beginning of the discrete music programme in the centre, there had been a tendency for the generalist teachers to view the music specialist as separate from the main programme. Two of the musicians commented on the isolation that could be experienced by being seen as an expert and at least one took active steps to facilitate music having a more inclusive role in the daily life of the centre (Chapter 4). The third musician was engrossed in her music and there were two unexpected consequences that arose during her time at the centre that were totally unplanned. One was the *The Magic Flute* project, which became a whole-of-centre enthusiasm, and the other was the children's choir, which occurred under her watch but was not initiated by her. As the children's choir project grew, members of the generalist staff became increasingly involved with the researcher-conductor, whose own position had also grown and become more visible and participatory. The very existence and projection of the children's choir was an example of an emerging story and was not a brainchild of any participants. This was in contrast to the adult singing group that had inspired the children. At no time did the adults in the singing group move beyond being an enterprise instructed by the music specialist, and the long-term effect on the staff was not to lead to a more inclusive music presence across the centre.

There was no perceived ownership of the children's choir and this led to a breakdown of barriers between the musician and generalist teachers. By the end of the first year, one of the generalist educators had not only taken a leading role in some performances, but had also become the music teacher in the centre, after the third musician resigned to go overseas. Other staff members started offering musical skills they had acquired – for example, playing piano and flute. This was the strongest indication that there was a movement around the idea of specialist knowledge and shared participation. As one of the initial aims of the research undertaken at this centre was to explore the role of specialists (Chapter 2), this development was unexpected and fascinating.

8

THE CHILD'S VOICE

Introduction

This chapter describes the children's musical learning, documented by using learning stories (Carr, 2001). Learning stories, or learning narratives, were originally developed for the early childhood context. They were designed as a sociocultural tool to support New Zealand's curriculum framework, *Te Whariki* (NZMOE, 1996), and have been adopted internationally. The learning story approach, to frame and record children's learning, has become popular in recent years. Carr (2001) derived the concept from Bruner's notion of narrative to record and analyse children's emerging stories about their own learning (Bruner, 1975). Bruner's view of narrative is that it constitutes ways of knowing. The authors of this book have previously investigated learning stories as a way of recording and interpreting young children's explorations of music (e.g., Acker, 2010; Nyland and Ferris, 2009). A major purpose of learning stories is to make children's learning visible. To further unpack the events described in this book, we now present five examples of learning stories of the ELC children engaged in musical explorations. Each example is taken from one of the above five chapters to explicate the musical experiences contained to indicate the value of these activities for individual children. For Chapters 3, 4, 5 and 6, we offer a learning story of an individual child and for Chapter 7 – the chapter on the children's chorus – we have recorded a learning story of a group of children collaborating and sharing knowledge.

As background, learning stories are introduced as a method of documentation and analysis of children's experiences. Cultural activity theory and the notion of affordances are also discussed as a means of theorising the children's learning. We then present the five learning stories and conclude with a discussion about the children as protagonists in the music programme in the ELC.

Learning stories

Learning stories have become an increasingly popular method of documenting and assessing children's learning and have been widely used at the ELC. For teachers, this storytelling technique involves observation, participation, involvement of children and their families and a means to share and develop relationships (Acker, 2008). Learning stories are seen as formative assessment as they document everyday events and discover the significance of these through an analytical frame based on identified learning dispositions. These dispositions are: taking an interest; being involved; persisting with difficulty; expressing an idea or feeling; and taking responsibility. Sequences of learning stories can provide a picture into children's learning and growing understanding.

Learning stories are a means of studying everyday experience. By documenting and exploring experience the participants are given a voice. In the learning story, it is not just what children say and do: actions and words are explored for meaning. There is no end product with a learning story, only the opportunity to reflect on what happened and how this might appear in other, more complex, ways in the future. Increasingly they are used for research (Podmore, 2006). The learning stories have three main sections. The first is the story, which may be recorded as a written anecdote, a photographic sequence or event, or a transcript of a conversation. The second element is the analysis of the story, which explores the story and identifies what learning dispositions created this particular scenario. The strength of this approach to storytelling and analysis is that it is contextual and, therefore, includes all actors who have participated, instead of concentrating on a decontextualised individual, as previous observation methods often did in early childhood (Rinaldi, 2006). The third essential element of the learning story is the examination of the story, the context and the learner's/s' actions to reflect on the potential of the particular situation.

For early childhood researchers, observations are usually shared between the centre and events that may occur outside with the family. There may be more than one observer contributing and participants are often invited to add perspective. For example, the learning story presented here from Chapter 5 clearly indicates the home and centre role in producing the event recorded. The focus in this type of observation is on learning, making learning visible, learning dispositions, learning in social and physical contexts and the potential for learning. The examples provided here are snapshots, but already the potential to include others and extend the children's learning is clearly stated. A value of this type of enquiry is that the gaze brought to bear on the story is an intense and detailed one. As Robertson (2006) says, 'we can see the minutiae of experiences' (p. 152). The flexibility of learning stories, with the possibility of revisiting, means we can constantly reflect, recall and find new meanings and messages in the stories.

We are of the opinion that learning stories are an appropriate way to record children's musical experiences, as one aspect of music and narrative enquiry that is mentioned by researchers is the importance of relationships. Such an emphasis is supported by the socio/cultural approach (Rogoff, 2003; Vygotsky, 1978) to experiences with music that have been discussed in this book. In each observation presented here, it was the presence of the music that helped create a relationship between the participants.

The information collected in the learning story and the learning dispositions are a guide to reviewing what has happened. We also reinterpret this information using the idea of affordances (Forman, 1994; Needham, 2007) to examine the learning that took place as a guide to future activities. In this way, the existing understandings of the children, levels of participation, the environment and potential of the learning culture can all become part of the conversation. The centre as a developmental niche (Super and Harkness, 1986) consists of the social, physical, cultural and historical aspects of experience, as introduced in Chapter 2. Language, including music, is a mediator of learning and accomplishment. As we observe children's participation within the context and record and interpret their activities as learning stories, we are able to comment on their relationship with the music in the centre, their own individual learning and preferences and the music programme as a whole. Carr comments on the use of Bruner's notion of narrative, the idea of socially mediated learning dispositions:

> the label 'learning narratives' has been employed because, as Bruner (1975) argued, they add the deontic (this is what you're usually supposed to do) and the possible (this is what you could do if the occasion is right) to the epistemic (this is what you do here) quality of a script. They are dispositional, and less local. But, like scripts, they provide one way of mapping the terrain between the individual and the sociocultural environment of the early childhood setting or the classrooms, the mediated action, and thereby help us to better both the individual learner and the learning environment. (Carr, 2000, p. 62)

The idea of affordances, also included here, suggests that it is through action that children perceive their environment. In this case we are discussing children's engagement with music as a cultural activity within a particular context. The children were introduced to cultural artefacts in the form of song, instruments, recorded music and opera, a choir, movement games and stories. The children were able to reinterpret their own experiences and we explore this through the following learning stories.

The learning story frame, as an interpretive tool, with affordances included, is shown in Table 8.1.

Example learning stories

In the following section of this chapter we present five learning stories from Chapters 3, 4, 5, 6 and 7. For Chapter 3 we describe a child who takes responsibility for her own pitch awareness and exploration. For Chapter 4, which tells the

TABLE 8.1 Learning story frame

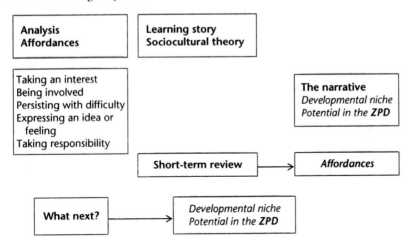

story of Leah, we recount an incident of dramatic play and for Kylie, in Chapter 5, we report on one child's enthusiasm for the Queen of the Night in *The Magic Flute*. Chapter 6 centred on Suzana as a home-room teacher, so this learning story has focused on the discussions she had with the children and one child's response. Finally, the children in the choir, Chapter 7, are shown working together; their understanding of the role of conductor clearly emerges.

Learning story, Lesley: mindful hands – the story of a point

Context

Lesley was particular about helping the children find an appropriate pitch for their singing voices. She often used her hand to guide the children towards pitch awareness and self-correction when they were singing. She never verbally corrected the children, but would sometimes suggest 'Let's start again shall we?'

The story

The children were singing with Lesley. The morning 'Hello' song had been sung, the children had looked with interest at the scene in the middle of the floor, which consisted of a green chiffon scarf with a brown furry scarf placed across the middle in a wavy line (this was the Yarra river), a plastic kookaburra and frog, plus a pair of finger cymbals. Around the edge was a series of instruments consisting of three glockenspiels, a xylophone, tone blocks, three of Lesley's recorders and three wooden flutes. Lesley had also left the book with lesson plans and sheet music lying on the floor. One of the girls in the group crawled over to the book and flipped through the pages. 'Sing this one,' she said, pointing to a page of music. Lesley concurred and the group stood up to sing 'The Earth is Our Mother'. As the children were singing, the little girl who had requested the song started to point in the air. Her points followed the pitch changes in the song.

The learning dispositions

Taking an interest

Finding an interest here: a topic, an activity, a role. Recognising the familiar, enjoying the unfamiliar, coping with change

The child had chosen the song, although doubtful if she could tell which one it was as this was chosen by pointing at the score. She was able to recognise the pitch changes and used her hand and finger intentionally to indicate this. Gestures are taken here as communicative language acts (Lock, 1980) and the cognition indicated in the child's pointing hand are representative of her interest and engagement, making visible her understanding of the musical concept of pitch.

Being involved

Paying attention for a sustained period, feeling safe, trusting others. Being playful with others and/or materials

Level of involvement was high in that the child facilitated the singing of the song, was engaged in the singing beyond the activity of singing words to include a musical understanding of pitch and use a body movement to represent this knowledge. To take a leadership role in choosing material and have such a participatory voice, through gesture, within the activity suggests a sense of belonging and trust.

Persisting with difficulty

Setting and choosing difficult tasks. Using a range of strategies to solve problems when 'stuck'
   N/A

Expressing an idea or feeling

In a range of ways – for example, oral language, gesture, music, art, writing etc.

This incident was an example of the dialectical unity between thought and speech (the gesture). The gesture was repeated, changing as the pitch changed and, therefore, an informed and expressive statement. The idea of pitch was clearly conveyed to those present and the child's knowledge of this element was assured.

Taking responsibility

Responding to others, to stories and imagined events, ensuring that things are fair, self-evaluating, helping others, contributing to programme

The knowledge and learning displayed by this child suggests a sensitivity to the messages of others in that she has been able to adopt a strategy of the musician, Lesley, to physically place her voice in a song. She has been observant, has understood the meaning of Lesley's gestures and has been able to use her own version in a purposeful way to resolve her own performance, thus self-evaluating. She has contributed to the group through asking for the song and then using an external mediator that can be seen and, therefore, shared with others.

Comment

The last two sections of a learning story contain a review of the learning; to get a better view of the context we have considered the affordances of the situation here. Music is a language of childhood and an expression of culture. Affordances focus on what knowledge is constructed by actors in relation to constraints or enabling elements in the environment. Different activities, materials or artefacts offer different potential for children to explore and experiment with ideas and theories (Carr, 2000). Forman suggests that some experiences are more suitable for theory testing and some for theory making (1994).

In the above narrative, the child was engaged in a cultural activity within a particular context. As a cultural artefact, 'The Earth is My Mother' is a complex song – musically and philosophically. Lesley introduced the song as a result of her interest in nature and the significance she placed on relationships with the natural world. The children's response was intuitive, as if they understood the importance of the song to Lesley. The words were soft and the melody lilting, something that requires even, sustained breathing and an ability to hold a note. The child was responding to these challenges by using Lesley's actions to mediate her own pitch, thus suggesting her own relationship with Lesley and the music was strong; there was an opportunity to display a competence not expected in a child this age (the Banksia group were between the ages of three and four).

Another aspect of the environment that can be considered is the idea of the context as a developmental niche with opportunities for children to construct knowledge in the zone of proximal development (ZPD) (Vygotsky, 1978). Young (2008b) has studied children making music and commented on the value of non-verbal language as a useful way to add meaning to an exchange. Lesley's physical representation of pitch by pointing was a way of helping this child access the concept of pitch and gain mastery over the idea, supporting Young's idea that 'a tendency to import language-derived versions of collaboration as templates for understanding children's collaboration has obscured processes intrinsic to the act of music making' (2008b, p. 3). Use of space and time has been commented upon in earlier chapters of this book and this story is an example of the power of actions, or gestures, as a means of musical expression that was welcomed in this environment.

Learning story, Leah: spontaneous music

Context

Having been the music specialist in the arts programme at the ELC for some time, Leah left to travel to South America. On her return, she agreed to a request by the director to be a travelling musician, taking music to the home-rooms in the centre. The following story reflects a more spontaneous and child-directed approach than Leah had experienced in the music sessions. She was able to enjoy observing these incidents, which gave her insights into children's ideas and the knowledge they brought into the programme.

The learning story

Today, one of the children brought in a small karaoke machine. Although the room teacher felt that this was a commercial toy and that others would not be attracted by it, it drew an instant interest from a small group of children, as they ran to set themselves up on the outdoor wooden stage. Some children sang individually, some shared the microphone, some just observed.

N (4), a confident singer, sang a gospel song 'The Ocean Refuses No River'.

> The ocean refuses no river, no river.
> The ocean refuses no river, no river.
> Alleluia, Allelu, Aaaaaalleluia.
> Alleluia, Allelu, Aaaaalleluia.

She enquired if this could be video-recorded. The educator suggested that this could be done later and suggested that N should enjoy her 'performance'. N's singing was competent, in line with the gospel style, tuneful and rhythmic, as she moved her feet, sideways, to the beat. When finished, her 'audience' gave her a big applause. The children decided to play a chasing game, leaving a newly arrived boy with the machine. He did not speak much English, but seemed interested in N's song as he was observing and smiling at her. He waited for his turn and then carefully explored the karaoke machine. He picked up the microphone and started to make unusual sounds that varied in volume, character, pitch and pattern. This attracted N's attention, who then turned to the 'stage' and took the role of audience. After a while, he offered her the microphone. N smiled and said: 'We could both sing "Alleluia".' The boy smiled back, but shook his head 'no': 'Sing.'

The learning dispositions

Taking an interest

Finding an interest here: a topic, an activity, a role. Recognising the familiar, enjoying the unfamiliar, coping with change

The karaoke machine was of interest to a group of the children in the Waratah room. The machine was a familiar artefact that suggested performance to the children and N was a competent singer who could sing a song from beginning to end. Completing a solo performance of a song is a slightly unusual skill in this age group. N also wanted to be recorded, so she was aware of the permanence of a video recording. She held her audience throughout the song and was then able to change tack and become an audience and then a collaborator.

Being involved

Paying attention for a sustained period, feeling safe, trusting others. Being playful with others and/or materials

Involvement is an important facet of well-being (Laevers, 2011) and the attention sustained across the events here suggest the child N felt trust and could, therefore, perform for her friends. She was also able to change role to that of audience, becoming a collaborator to the extent that she asked the other child to become a performer. He smiled as he refused the invitation. This exchange had no prescribed goal. The karaoke machine was the focus while actions emerged spontaneously as the children played.

Persisting with difficulty

Setting and choosing difficult tasks. Using a range of strategies to solve problems when 'stuck'

N's strategy of being interested in the boy's sound-making but not understanding it as a formal noise like her song was to invite him to perform her song with her. She was happy to share and to understand the activity framed it with the 'Alleluia' song.

Expressing an idea or feeling

In a range of ways – for example, oral language, gesture, music, art, writing etc.

There were a number of ideas expressed in this incident. Through her performance, N was able to express her understanding of the karaoke machine and also her own ideas of appropriate music for such a vehicle. This was evidenced when she invited the little boy to join her in song. She was acknowledging his use of the microphone and sound-making, and wanted to bring this into a form she could use. The request for the recording also suggests an understanding of the ephemeral nature of music as opposed to forms of the arts like painting or sculpture. She could see that her song would be gone once she had finished singing; this is a sophisticated understanding of levels of impermanence. This indicates a high degree of symbol use.

Taking responsibility

Responding to others, to stories and imagined events, ensuring that things are fair, self-evaluating, helping others, contributing to programme

N was a willing leader and collaborator. She led the way in the exploration of the karaoke machine and the other children acknowledged her competence by rewarding her performance with a clap. She was happy to share with the little boy, who appeared to be a novice, and she offered him a frame in which they could work together. She contributed to her own learning and that of the other children; her manner was fair and, at times, playful.

Comment

The affordances that were present in this narrative were, most notably, the toy karaoke machine. The children were familiar with this artefact and acknowledged its competent use by N. The little boy seemed to be a novice, but this might have been more about his own abilities and confidence as a sound-maker. The educator was dismissive of the machine as a toy and also did not want to video the singing, but did offer to do so later. There was, therefore, an atmosphere of tolerance that made the children's independent explorations possible.

An artefact, such as the machine, is embedded with all sorts of cultural activity within the wider social context. Niland's research (2012) discusses children's use of the karaoke in great detail. Children who watched television shows, like *The Voice*, brought a knowledge of karaoke from popular culture that was dominant in this play. This can be seen in the spontaneous performance and the clapping. In this way, the dominance of a particular cultural understanding might even, according to Forman (1994), limit children's experimentation as they had a perception of karaoke already that did not invite theory making or testing. The little boy, with little experience of English, experimented in a less obvious way. Therefore, the music that arose from the karaoke toy was a known song, from the choir repertoire, sung by one of the children. The other use of the toy was experimenting with different types of sounds. In this case, the little boy's explorations were possibly more interesting, but also taken by N as a less informed use.

Learning story, Kylie: R and The Magic Flute *– communicating with the family*

Context

The following learning story was included in a parent questionnaire sent home to R's parents when a research paper on her involvement with the *Magic Flute* project was being prepared (Nyland *et al.*, 2011). The questionnaire consisted of general questions about the parents' knowledge of the music programme at the ELC and, included at the end, was the learning story below.

We introduced the story to the parents in the following way:

> The following learning story is a popular early childhood method of assessing children's learning. They are especially valuable when there are many voices

in the story. We would like to share this story with you and invite you to record your reactions. (Questionnaire, 3 November 2010)

The learning story

The children were sitting with Suzana and Kylie. Suzana was sharing a collaborative drawing the children had done of the Queen of the Night (see Figure 5.2). She had also written down the remarks the children had made about the Queen and she commented that R had been singing the Queen's song to her friends. The children in the group looked at R, who started singing the first phrases of the Queen of the Night aria. The children, Suzana and Kylie applauded.

After the singing, Kylie described the song as a sad one and an angry one. R responded: 'She was worried. She thought Sarastro might keep her forever ... but the Prince was coming ... the Prince was coming to save her.' On this last phrase she waved her finger in the air.

Kylie then talked about the costumes, costume change and the fact that when she, Kylie, sings opera she wears different costumes. One child commented that when the singers change costumes they change their voices. Kylie then suggested the group watch the next part of the opera and the children readily agreed, crying out: 'Yes!'

Learning story analysis

Taking an interest

Finding an interest here: a topic, an activity, a role. Recognising the familiar, enjoying the unfamiliar, coping with change

The interest here was the Queen of the Night; the children, with Suzana, had brought their collaborative drawing of the Queen to share with Kylie. This was a familiar experience for the children. The unfamiliar, commented upon by Suzana, was R trying to find a head voice and sing the Queen's aria. The unfamiliar was greeted with applause.

Being involved

Paying attention for a sustained period, feeling safe, trusting others. Being playful with others and/or materials

R's rendition of the Queen's aria suggested sustained attention. She was familiar with the style of the singing, some of the pitch changes and the overall feeling. To perform like this indicates she felt safe and trusting as she was playing with musical elements of a song very publicly.

Persisting with difficulty

Setting and choosing difficult tasks. Using a range of strategies to solve problem when 'stuck'

Singing in front of peers, in a pretend way that is more akin to play than performance, would be considered a challenging task for a young child. The context (the music session) and the shared interest in *The Magic Flute* (a vicarious experience and a fairy story) enabled R to improvise after the first few phrases of the song. The children recognised her accomplishment through their applause.

Expressing an idea or feeling

In a range of ways – for example, oral language, gesture, music, art, writing etc.

There were a number of expressive modes in this story. The collaborative drawing of the Queen of the Night indicates the children saw her as a glamorous woman with long eyelashes. R sang, gestured and verbally explained why the Queen was sad. To perceive an adult as worried is a sign of how powerful a fairy story can be in taking children into a different world.

Taking responsibility

Responding to others, to stories and imagined events, ensuring that things are fair, self-evaluating, helping others, contributing to programme

R was taking responsibility for her own learning by being so interested that she became an informed participant in the story and the music. Her response to Kylie's comments about the Queen's song being a sad one is indicative of thoughtfulness, suggesting an understanding of story, even though she did have a misplaced sympathy for the Queen.

Comment

R's parents were pleased with the information about R contained in this observation and, in their written response to the questionnaire (3 November 2010), they reported that:

> It's difficult to get R to tell us about what she does at ELC in general. When we ask she mostly says 'Nothing'. But she did tell us about *Magic Flute*, about the characters and the story, and, of course, sang the Queen of the Night aria for us. It is an activity at ELC that has stood out for her. She came home one afternoon and Jeanette asked her if she wanted to watch TV, and R said 'No, I want to watch *The Magic Flute* on YouTube'.

The parents were enthusiastic about the arts programme and saw the music as a valuable part of the educational practices at the centre.

> Music is important for R's development because she learns to appreciate music, by both listening and playing/singing, which is a rewarding and enriching experience. It engages a young mind and evokes emotional and

spiritual reactions that reading or playing cannot. Music involves both physical co-ordination and 'mental gymnastics', which is (I'm told) good for mental development.

The comments from the parents on the questionnaire, and specifically about the learning story, were useful in ascertaining that R had shared the project with her parents; they were enthusiastic about music in the programme. The parents were articulate about the value of music for their child and the comment about the television emphasises R's enthusiasm for the particular project. It also highlights the different ways that basic technology, like YouTube, can now bring a great variety of music into homes and centres. This encourages experiences like this crossing the borders between home and the early childhood setting.

Learning story, Suzana: L on the 'Symphony of Dead Animals'

The story

There had been a dramatic storm the night before this story took place. Suzana was encouraging the children to think about the natural world in a sustainable and ecological way. The children were writing their memories of the storm as music and Suzana had given them manuscript paper with a treble clef to facilitate recording their feelings about the storm. One child, L, called his 'The Yarra River Storm Music' and did a dark scribble. L recorded his ideas in Figure 8.1.

Suzana recorded his description of his ideas for the drawing underneath. 'A symphony for dead animals in the river after the storm. It's a music for instrument called human voice.'

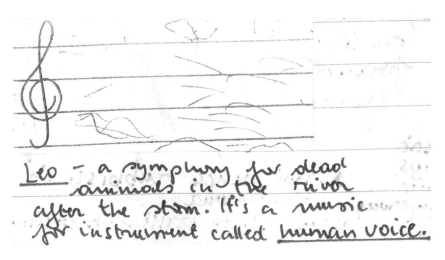

FIGURE 8.1 L's symphony

Learning story analysis

Taking an interest

Finding an interest here: a topic, an activity, a role. Recognising the familiar, enjoying the unfamiliar, coping with change

L's reaction to the activity of exploring the storm through music was probably unexpected. The characteristics of this particular storm were heavy rain, wind, fallen trees and a blackout. There was no flooding, so L's emphasis on animals presumably comes from images of other storms; he was bringing out the aspect of storms that had most affected him – the plight of the vulnerable. He brought in the river (familiar territory for children of the ELC), took the word 'symphony' and used it in a poetical way to name his drawing.

Being involved

Paying attention for a sustained period, feeling safe, trusting others. Being playful with others and/or materials

The adding of knowledge of previous storms, or floods, to the activity of remembering and expressing the storm of the night before suggests sustained thought over a period of time. He was in a safe context where he could bring up the idea of death associated with storms and the adult, Suzana, respected this contribution and recorded it in the curriculum book. He was also being playful in the way he used the words: symphony for dead animals, river, after the storm, instrument and human voice – in terms of 'playing' with the words rather than the way we often view children's play. L's choice of words is almost like an elegy.

Persisting with difficulty

Setting and choosing difficult tasks. Using a range of strategies to solve problems when 'stuck'

The protagonist in this story was Suzana, who planned to discuss the storm with the children and guide their expression of the event into a music score, a somewhat oblique form of expression for very young children even if familiar with the idea of the score. L's meeting of the challenge was interesting and multilayered.

Expressing an idea or feeling

In a range of ways – for example, oral language, gesture, music, art, writing etc.

L used a variety of media to express his feelings. Perhaps the most expressive idea was the choice of the topic. Certainly the topic of dead animals was one that would be noticed by others and have the potential to create emotional feelings in others. L's words were poetic and the strength of the ideas within the individual words and phrases was striking. The drawing itself is graphic. There is movement in the lines.

It seems as if the stave is the river and the horizontal lines are the animals being swept down river by the storm.

Taking responsibility

Responding to others, to stories and imagined events, ensuring that things are fair, self-evaluating, helping others, contributing to programme

L emerges as a child who is thoughtful and serious. His response to the challenge to think about the storm was profound. He was able to link previous knowledge of storms with the storm of the night before. He has also included the river, which has been such a prominent feature in many of the ELC stories.

Comment

This learning story is an example of Suzana utilising an intentional teaching approach and the response she has elicited from the child L. L's association with the storm and the death of animals is not one most adults would like to think of as worrying a child. Some may even have tried to distract him and, therefore, not accepted his offering. The opportunity to express his ideas in words and pictures and have these recorded as important makes the ELC, Suzana and the invitation to share his thoughts an enabling feature of the environment in this learning story.

L, as he appears in this story, is a child who thinks deeply about the world, is expressive and can use different media to express different aspects of his ideas. His drawing is full of movement, suggesting enormous strength as the animals are swept across the stave. This is a result of the storm, so he is able to record the devastation of a storm here. Drawing is one of the most open media, as flights of imagination can happen with drawings. For young children, a drawing might be able to express something they cannot verbally express. Staff members from the centre frequently ask children to draw after a music session. This was discussed in Chapter 3. In L's words, which accompanied the drawing, he was able to express a tribute – one that could be performed using the 'human voice' – and he was able to theorise the voice as an instrument. The majestic word 'symphony' was given to him by Suzana; this was used to give gravitas to the concepts he was exploring.

Learning story: the choir

The story

The Blue Gum room children and their teachers went on their regular visit to the local river, where they explored different plants and inhabitants. At one stage, a small group of girls got together and decided to perform one of their favourite songs, 'Celebrate the Rain', which is an original piece written by one of the music specialists at the centre.

FIGURE 8.2 Singing by the river

> Celebrate the rain falling down
> Celebrate the green trees growing from the ground
> Celebrate the new paradise we've found
> Celebrate the rain falling down.

The children had been introduced to the concept of conducting in their previous choir-practice session. A (4) picked up a stick and conducted. The group were responsive, including reading A's cues to change the dynamics and tempo. The teacher recorded this event on video, which the children have had the opportunity to revisit.

Learning story analysis

Taking an interest

Finding an interest here: a topic, an activity, a role. Recognising the familiar, enjoying the unfamiliar, coping with change

FIGURE 8.3 Conducting

A variety of interests came together as affordances to make this event possible. The children shared a favourite song because the ELC had established a choir/singing group. They were by the river, which was a terrain with which they were familiar, that they had used often for different types of exploration. The knowledge of a conductor and his/her role for the choir was recent. The decision to sing the song together moved the children into less familiar territory; then A brought the group together by adopting a new role.

Being involved

Paying attention for a sustained period, feeling safe, trusting others. Being playful with others and/or materials

Involvement was expressed in a number of ways; the children's capacity to plan and carry out the group venture was an indication of previous knowledge of the song, the choir standing together and the watching of the conductor. These all indicated previous sustained attention to gain these skills. If Figure 8.2 is examined, we can see from A's positioning and the stick in her right hand that she is about to start the song. The four standing on the fallen log are watching closely for their cue – a disciplined joint activity.

Persisting with difficulty

Setting and choosing difficult tasks. Using a range of strategies to solve problems when 'stuck'

The children have chosen a difficult task that requires careful attention, with knowledge of performance, of the song and how to follow a novice conductor. Their shared knowledge, commitment to the task and A's competence make this complex task possible.

Expressing an idea or feeling

In a range of ways – for example, oral language, gesture, music, art, writing etc.

This occurs in a number of ways. The song itself, as a favourite, is indicative of a shared interest in the natural world and a sympathy, or liking, of the natural world. The children, by the river, will celebrate the rain through song. The different roles of chorister and conductor are clearly expressed.

Expressing an idea or feeling

In a range of ways – for example, oral language, gesture, music, art, writing etc.

Ideas are expressed in this story through music, gesture, physical positioning and joint planning, which combined to bring about a situation where children were able to use all these languages for the joint purpose of celebrating nature – the rain. Rain is extremely important in Australia as it is largely desert. This interest and enthusiasm for rain could also have been strengthened through adult interest in weather patterns and, therefore, have cultural meaning.

Taking responsibility

Responding to others, to stories and imagined events, ensuring that things are fair, self-evaluating, helping others, contributing to programme

A group of children planned and enacted a collaborative activity that required knowledge of a song, of group singing and different roles within a choir. They were disciplined and followed the lead of the self-selected conductor. The conductor – through her positioning in front of the group, her hand positions, as observed in the photo, her initiative in finding a baton quickly and her obvious control of the group – and each of the members of the group were able to be responsible for the planned action. The children themselves created their plan to sing their song together, they chose the song and it was apposite for the site they were singing in. When A stepped into a leadership role, there was an implicit

understanding the choristers would follow her lead, as this would make the collaborative effort successful.

Comment

Conducting is a musical language that unifies a group through the reading of visible
gestures. As in this observation, these gestures interpret the music by instructing the
performers on such musical elements as tempo, duration, dynamics, rhythm, beat
and colour. This is highly individualised activity that is very public. The conductor
must overtly instruct the singers and be creative by interpreting the meaning of the
song. The interpretation was communicated through meaningful musical elements.
The children stood on the log to be a choir and this action inspired A to extend the
choir-concept by picking up a stick and becoming a conductor. Although she was
physically below them, she now became a powerful figure because of the role she
had adopted. Her hand movements were indicative of her understanding of the
mood of the song and she clearly remembered the conducting model presented
previously; she managed to convey musical messages to the singers so they could act
in unison. She did this with both hands.

Conclusion

In this chapter we have dug down into the data to take a more detailed look at the
children and their understandings and learning. This has been done using the tool
of learning stories, which were developed to record and analyse children's experiences in a more social/cultural/historical/contextual way. The children's learning
dispositions were identified in order to see what learning took place, what was possible in the situation and to evaluate the incidents for future possibilities.

Each learning story was based on one of Chapters 3–7 and was representative of
the musician, educator or particular initiative. For Lesley, we took the story of the
child pointing. Lesley's use of spontaneous gesture to discover a suitable key for the
children to sing in and to assist in the singing was dominant in our observations. The
child who adopted this method of pitch recognition and control ably illustrated
Lesley's non-verbal methods of teaching. The next narrative was about Leah; here
we chose to emphasise her trips around the rooms, where she was able to observe
children's musical competence through the lens of spontaneous play. As Leah was
interested in community singing, the role of music in everyday life and the children's explorations of the toy karaoke machine were selected. Kylie did many formal
music activities with the children and the project that took over the centre for a
short while, and attracted the interest of parents because of the children's enthusiasm, was the *Magic Flute* investigation. The learning story presented here also contains the parent voice. For Suzana, we examined her 2010 curriculum book for an
event that was representative of one of her teaching strategies. Here we found her
records of the children exploring a natural event, a wild storm they had experienced
the night before. Suzana prompted them to express the storm as a symphony. The

child L's response was a timely reminder that children are also exposed to the thoughts and anxieties of the adult world. Finally, with the choir, it was fitting to introduce a collaborative incident designed and carried through by the children themselves. A choir is a disciplined way of working together and these children accomplished this discipline in their rendition of 'Celebrate the Rain'.

One aspect of these learning stories worth a mention was the role of play. From the ancient world through to today, children and theories of play have been promulgated. On the question of play, Brown and Patte (2013) comment that 'play' is an easy phenomenon to recognise, but a hard one to define. In the stories above there are a number of instances where play is the driving force of the child's ability and motivation to explore in depth a particular concept or concepts. The child pointing was remembering a model and trying it out for herself, spontaneously, in a context where she was relaxed. The children experimenting with the karaoke machine were more traditionally engaged in pretend and dramatic play. Their play was also embedded in cultural knowledge they brought to the event. For R and the Queen of the Night, the interest was possibly spurred by the emotional magic of the fairy story. Certainly, the child was able to achieve an unusual feat that was driven by a deep interest. For L, the play could be seen in the strength of his view of the storm and the way he was able to express this through wordplay and expressive lines. Here, with all these children, Vygotsky's metaphor that when children play they are a 'head taller' (1978, p. 102) could be evidenced. In the last story, the children were engaging in social play where they had a negotiated goal, a knowledge of the choir and conductors – a shared objective made possible the performance observed.

In the next chapter, the last, we revisit the aims of our research from Chapter 1 and pull out the major themes that have merged across the stories told in this book. Most importantly, we give a voice to the director, in relation to the aims and themes, as the designer of the arts programme and an instigator, through her belief in the arts, of the use of space, time, aesthetics and tradition.

PART III

Conclusion

9

REVISITING AND CONCLUDING REMARKS

Introduction

In this book we have told the story of a journey, undertaken by a community in an early childhood centre, searching for possibilities for music within an active arts programme. After exploring the historical context of arts education and music education in early childhood settings in Australia, we explained the particular context of the ELC with which we have been involved. We have documented the ways in which the music programme has evolved in the ten years during which the research took place. The process has been an integral part of the centre's overall research interest in curriculum approaches and the music programme was consequently underpinned by common theoretical threads that gave the music enterprise integrity within the centre's curriculum. The director, as the participant who designed the arts programme and initiated the music research project, was of the opinion that no one theoretical approach to curriculum would do, but rather that aspects of different approaches would illuminate their work and suggest ways to develop. This willingness to accept the changing possibilities ensured that the programme evolved in an organic way. This is why we have a story that shifts and changes complexion, according to the particular passions, skills and interests of the musicians and teachers who have chosen the directions in which to take the music programme.

In Part I of this book we established the contexts that frame the story. We considered the nature and role of the arts and of music in early childhood, both in contemporary Australia and historically. We have examined the particular context of the ELC with which we were involved, as the nature of the centre clearly influenced and shaped the way the events developed. This context included the carefully crafted physical environment and the social and cultural climate, as well as the education environment peculiar to this centre. This was a research centre, where research regarding curriculum was a fundamental driver for educational endeavours.

The history of the ELC's emerging research interests regarding curriculum, along with the curriculum projects and ideas that were informed by this research, have been presented. The story of the music in the centre was an essential part of this overarching view. Given the centre director's commitment to the notion that the arts are a fundamental component of an effective early childhood programme, the arts, including music, were, at times, both a stimulus for research at the centre and served by research.

In Part II, we have followed the practice of three musicians who worked with the children in their own individual and particular ways. In these chapters, the voice of the musicians is clear, and is the lens through which we tell the story. We also document the work of one home-room teacher who became closely involved with the possibilities arising from the work of the third musician, in this case providing the perspective of a generalist teacher. The penultimate chapter in this section describes a project in which one researcher participated actively, collaborating with the teachers and two of the musicians to initiate a centre-wide singing project that attracted strong attention from the parents. Here the perspective is complex and interconnected. The last chapter in this part of the book examines children's experiences, through the use of learning stories. This perspective allows a close-grained, detailed view of the children as learners during some of the music activities, and makes their learning visible in rich ways.

In Part III we draw conclusions, attempting to follow threads and broad ideas through the narrative. The protagonists in this journey were drawn from all aspects of the ELC's programme. The children, the musicians, the educators, the director and the parents were all part of this research. Their activities were within an environment established by the centre's overall philosophy and curriculum approaches. The ELC's director, as the educational leader, has been responsible for the establishment and maintenance of the centre's characteristic approaches and has upheld and driven the research that informed the curriculum and the programme. She has also shaped the sense of physical and aesthetic space that is clear throughout the centre. As an advocate for the power of the arts in early childhood education, along with her long-term involvement as leader of the centre, she provides a very significant perspective to the research described here. For these reasons, we chose to ask the director to reflect on the themes that have emerged from the documentation of the music programme during the time we have recorded it. All citations in this chapter come from an in-depth interview with the director, held at the end of the writing process, unless otherwise indicated.

In this chapter we, therefore, return to the aims identified in Chapter 1 to frame the chapter and discuss the meanings that have emerged, as well as how these events might influence future practice in the centre. There are also messages that could be generalised to other early childhood services and settings. The aims as identified in Chapter 1 are listed below and we take these as the basic categories in which to sum up and discuss findings.

The aims in this book were to:

- Reaffirm children's communicative competence when exposed to high-quality musical experiences
- Provide new perspectives on children's ability to engage with music in many diverse forms
- Explore and promote to role of the musician as artist/teacher
- Support an argument that the arts are an important part of human experience and should be accorded citizenship rights in early childhood programmes.

Aim 1: children's competence and the quality of experience

The discussion of this aim has a dual focus. One is the image of the competent, communicative child; the other is the question of the quality of experience. To address this dual focus and to contextualise the idea of children's competence being enhanced in enabling environments, we have divided the discussion into the following points: the value of the project approach; the medium of music itself as a language and cultural and cognitive tool; the director's approach to the significance of different modes of expression; and, finally, the careful planning that was invested in the design of the environment and curriculum.

Projects

The educators in this book had decided to pursue a project approach with the children within a curriculum that encouraged critical enquiry, discovery and creativity. Many of the projects that were observed have been mentioned in this book and a few aspects of some of these projects have been unpacked. These projects were formally adopted by the centre and some had an external driver, as in Let're Verde, or the United Nations annual themes. Others were embedded in the locality of the centre, which made great use of the nearby river, the old convent and the Children's Farm. These explorations in turn led to a constant underlying theme of sustainability and respect for nature. Other projects developed spontaneously, as seen with *The Magic Flute*. Within the projects there were examples of children's ability to enquire into complex stories, like the Antarctic exploration where the connectedness between staff at Casey Base and the children in Melbourne created an exciting exploratory space that led to creative work, which is illustrated in the story *Melt* and the 'Diamond Dust' song.

Projects were designed to provide an opportunity for children to have in-depth investigations into topics of interest and in turn develop deeper understandings and insights into the events they encountered. Projects assist children to theorise about their world, to help develop their own curriculum. In this book there have been a number of examples of this phenomenon. The director referred to projects as an 'exploration of big ideas with lots of hooks'.

I like the idea of big ideas. So *The Magic Flute* is a big idea for the children. Big ideas are not obvious choices. They're big ideas and those big ideas pushed children and teachers into much more interesting and exciting learning spaces. And then music, like if we talk about *The Magic Flute*; so there's the big idea and then there were a whole lot of hooks that were used by Kylie and Suzana to keep lifting the learning and the understanding. They were doing the drawings. That was one hook. Young children and music has also been a focus and an acknowledgement of music as a special language of childhood.

One way of searching for the big ideas was to utilise the arts as a language. Influenced by a combination of scholars – like Trevarthen (1998), who presents a case for language and culture; Eisner (2002), who seeks to promote the place of the arts in children's lives; and Reggio Emilia centres, which advocate for children's right to language and aesthetics (Edwards, Gandini and Forman, 1998) – the ELC's theorising about the arts was all encompassing.

Young children and music

The director discussed the idea of the importance of music in children's lives from birth.

> From birth, children communicate using gestures, sounds, language and assisted communications; you know, they are social beings who are intrinsically motivated to exchange ideas, thoughts, questions and feelings and to use a range of tools and media, including music. Music is the first one they say – music, dance and drama – to express themselves, connect with others and extend their learning.

In her interview, the director suggested that when children are engaged with a medium, like music, that is introducing them to creative expression and being provided with opportunities to create meaning themselves, then the learning they experience is 'holistic' and 'high quality'. She saw the musicians as providing 'a playful environment for children to explore music'. Play, she considered a 'joyful activity' and the children were able to 'willingly participate' in musical play. The director also saw the music as a vehicle to extend the multicultural nature of the programme in ways that were important to the children and families. She partly put this down to the driver in the Australian national early childhood framework, which has a strong multicultural and inclusive flavour to represent Australia's diverse population.

> There was an external driver there through the early years learning framework and government policy around inclusive practice. In the groups we have children with backgrounds from all over the world. Their families bring different musical experiences. So, for instance, just this year, a Greek child stood up in assembly and sang this song, with actions, in Greek. There's a

desire by many of the families to retain some of those old traditions through their musical culture. There is an overall educational commitment to retaining music as a cultural experience.

These ideas of musical play, multiculturalism, music as an expressive language from birth and the quality of experience led to an emphasis on modes of expression.

Modes of expression

The director was very committed to teaching and working with children using multi-modal tools. When discussing *The Magic Flute*, she described Kylie's approach as multi-modal and she thought this might have been partially due to Kylie's background in opera. 'Opera does play with costume, does play with set design, does draw on drama, does draw on gesture.' She developed her ideas on multi-model representation from the literature on Reggio Emilia. The emphasis on children as symbol-users and meaning-makers leads to multi-modal communications. This is a view that enables the idea that children can construct their own meanings of the world and their place in it. Children are active agents in their own learning, can express their discoveries and, through creative self-expression, can also co-construct knowledge with others. Eisner (2002) has been influential in how thinking has developed in the ELC around the arts as a language, as expressive and as taking many forms. Eisner states that the

> arts have an important role to play in refining our sensory system and cultivating our imaginative abilities. Indeed, the arts provide a kind of permission to pursue qualitative experience in a particularly focused way and to engage in the constructive exploration of what the imaginative process may engender. In this sense, the arts, in all their manifestations, are close in attitude to play. (p. 4)

This point about play was made in Chapter 8; the children's engagement in some of the activities was discussed at the end. The role of play in children's growth and development, and the role of languages in play are fundamental to early childhood philosophy and theory. In her own research into young children and dance, the director linked play and dance activities.

> Of interest also is how, when considering the notion of dance-play, children's independent problem-solving and decision-making shapes their intentional yet playful manipulation of movements to the point where thoughts and ideas become synonymous with the moving body.

In a lovely phrase, she says when thoughts and ideas become at one with the movement of the body 'it is at this point that the individual becomes the dance'. Reflecting on Eisner (2002) again, the director gives her explanation of the reason for using the arts, in all their forms, for working with young children: 'I would have to say that drawing on Eisner's works – as the arts being the creation of the mind – I was committed to the arts as facilitators of complex thinking, abstract thinking, symbolic thinking.' This relationship with the arts and the brain was an aim of the programme: for all children to have the opportunity to problem-solve as part of a creative process and have the joy of feeling they have worked out something special.

Planning for quality

The question of quality was a theme introduced under this first aim as well. The director gave many examples of careful planning to enhance children's experience. One of these, which has been frequently mentioned in these pages, is the attention to space, aesthetics and purpose.

> The Reggio Emilia work can be helpful here. So the aesthetically engineered environment actually supports the appreciation of the sound because the children go into the space and they know something beautiful is going to happen there. ... they are ready and willing and, interestingly, they are prepared to respect that. It's almost church-like. I think when someone is in the space with the music teacher, with beautiful music, it's sacred. It gives me goose bumps thinking about it.

She said of Lesley:

> For instance, she put a lot of effort to add to that environment from an aesthetic viewpoint. You know, the circle shape would always be established aesthetically through colour or texture and her instruments were laid out reverently. There was a sense of purpose there, you know, intent. And her object was to communicate the reverence that she felt for not only the instruments, but also the children – for the sound to the children. And that happened straight away, I think. So this is what high-quality music experience is.

Aim 2: the diversity of experience

The activities discussed here have been very diverse. The players themselves have had their own life histories, skills and approaches to music and relating to each other. The children's responses to the experiences offered depended on the moment, the topic and the form the experience took. Children had different tastes and desires which emanated as quite different understandings of the situation at hand. There were music sessions, which were a product of the individual musician and the children in each group, as well as the content chosen, which was a combination of musical tastes, beliefs about the centre curriculum, ideas of children's competence and the actual happenings on the day. Therefore, we witnessed singing, movement, use of instruments, listening, storytelling, looking, project explorations, dramatic play, visual expression and much more. These experiences took place in the designated special space, in the home-rooms, the outdoor area, the river, the Children's Farm and excursion sites, as well as the children's homes and family settings. As well as these physical settings, the children were encouraged into the world of digital technology that was used to complement, extend and, in some cases, make possible, some of the events observed.

The children, the different musicians and other adults have been described in the chapters of the book and a theme that has emerged is the use of technology. Lesley did, at times, use technology in a traditional way – for example, using CDs to support listening and movement activities. The director, however, has commented that Lesley's playing of her recorder – with its pure, direct sound – could be a metaphor for the 'pure' music she was aiming for in the centre programme. At the same time, she acknowledged that this was a question of Lesley's artistry and musicianship. Not everyone is able to use an instrument in this way.

> So they [children] pick up the recorder and just blow it, but that would not actually help them. So what we need is that expert teacher who can actually make those children feel a head taller in the Vygotskian sense. ZPD [zone of proximal development], set the ZPD, know that they all know sound; they all know sound, but do they know the pure sound and do they know this particular note and can they identify the different sounds as we go through the notes?

She acknowledged that each teacher brought 'their individuality to the craft of teaching'. She could identify a place for new technologies:

> So, on one level there were musical instruments; you said diverse forms – yes, well, we've had the piano, we've had recorder, we've had guitar, we've had percussion instruments, we've had voice, we've had voice (voice being very powerful), they've listened to recorded music, they've viewed YouTube. You know, it was interesting to see the shift from Lesley, who was a purist, to Kylie's time. There was a new generational influence. Kylie often used YouTube on the wall, so the children were experiencing the music in a variety of ways.

She identified technology as a new teaching tool.

> So, I think there's a vital force of responding to the knowledge explosion, new perspectives on children's ability to engage with diverse forms. The reality is that we now have access to such a wide array of opportunities across all disciplines. If we choose to learn something new today we can all just go to Google and find out stuff. So the flexibility that's available to us now with learning has influenced the teaching of music too.

The director considered these changes would occur naturally across the generations as new tools became available and those that grew up with these new literacies would use them purposively.

Aim 3: the role of the musician as artist/teacher

This third aim was one of the questions we asked ourselves when we first started visiting the music programme at the ELC. It has also emerged in concluding comments as one that the director is convinced was a cornerstone of their practice. This is against a background where many feel there has been a neglect of the arts, especially music.

For some time, educators in early childhood settings in Australia have found it difficult to provide good-quality music in their programmes. This unfortunate circumstance seems to be largely because teachers graduating from teacher education programmes at the country's universities are not equipped to work with children appropriately in this area. While most would agree that music is a significant part of a child's life, few feel competent to introduce any music into their programmes, let alone programmes likely to engage children at a high level. This appears to be the result of an unfortunate coincidence of trends. Once, applicants for early childhood education courses, usually young women, were likely to have learned to play the piano; as one of the genteel accomplishments, playing was not unusual, and certainly considered to be an advantage for anyone wanting to work with young children. In addition, young women were likely to be accustomed to singing, as part of their school education and perhaps as a result of belonging to church-going families. Teacher educators were, therefore, likely to be able to work with a cohort of students in their courses who had some grounding in music, or at least were disposed to consider that they needed to develop their skills in this area, and were able to design courses to extend on this base. Over the decades, these circumstances have become less likely. Social changes have meant that fewer young people have suitable musical skills: indeed, many are even quite uncomfortable with the idea of singing, feeling that singing is for others. Certainly, singing in front of a group of people is often considered confronting. At the same time, over the years, teacher training courses have been subject to a more crowded curriculum, and have been inclined to offer combined arts courses, which are unlikely to produce the skills, understanding, confidence and commitment to music that could result from stand-alone music courses. Over recent years, even the combined arts courses have, in most universities, contracted to one, or at the most, two semesters.

This is not to say that ELCs no longer value music as part of the curriculum, but, unless a centre is lucky enough to have a teacher who happens to be a good musician, they are obliged to look at other ways to provide this aspect of the curriculum than relying on the skills of each of their teachers. Some resort to arguably inadequate reliance on CDs, videos or YouTube, a practice unlikely to result in well-integrated and imaginative music-making. Some rely on voluntary, willing and musical parents, a solution which may work but is perhaps not reliable. Some employ specialist music companies from outside the centre, an expensive option which is also difficult to integrate into the programme.

The ELC that we have been discussing was, like other centres, caught in this dilemma. The director considered that this also applied to other the arts. She recalled that she was well aware that applicants for teaching positions at the centre were unlikely to be able to provide the kind of high-quality music, or, indeed, any kind of arts content for the children: 'When teachers were being employed ... I would ask "Can you play a musical instrument? Tell me about your artistic background," [and] there was nothing.' Furthermore, she was concerned that there seems to be no 'societal expectations around teachers coming out of teachers' programmes having learned the pure discipline knowledge of any of the arts forms. So it applies to dance, to drama, to visual art.'

The director's response to this dilemma was, as we have seen, to employ adults with skills and passion in arts areas to work with the children. In retrospect, she considered that, for the music programme, as with the other arts areas, this decision was vital: 'Now I think this whole idea of having artist musicians/teachers is the most important aspect of our approach to teaching right across the arts.' The decision to take this path coincided with the rise in interest in Australia in the Reggio Emilia approach, which supported the notion of employing artists in this way. This coincidence was serendipitous, providing a philosophical frame for what seemed to be a practical solution. The director felt that even without the influence of the Reggio Emilia approach she would have taken this path:

> And I think that if Reggio [Emilia] hadn't been happening at the same time that I came into the director role, I still would have done it, because I needed to have people who understood the purist discipline knowledge of those arts forms.

Benefits of the musician/teacher

Our narrative has followed the work of musician/teachers at the ELC over a ten-year period. In our concluding chapter, we are able to reflect on the benefits this experiment has provided for the centre's programme and community. These benefits appear to be quite clear. First, the musicians were able to impart their knowledge, skills and passion for music in the 'pure' way that director was seeking; second, the musicians introduced an extraordinary range of diverse content, skills and approaches that enriched both the children's lives and, in a more variable way, could influence the ways the class teachers thought about the possibilities of music in their programmes.

Purity

As a part of her view of the competent child, the director was an advocate for the child's capacity to be engaged by a high level of abstraction in the arts – by the purity of the arts. This experience was most likely to be provided by skilled musicians, actively involved as musicians in their own right. The director said the following about the value of providing music experiences as a discrete aspect of the arts programme:

> I think that recognising that music needed the time and the space to be experienced for its purity, you know, and not overtly cluttered with the other arts forms, is important. Because I think to tune children to sound in the first instance, pure sound, and then having the silence and the space to hear the melody and to recognise different pitches, are really important elements of experience, if you like. And focusing children's attention on them actually creates a more complete experience for the child.

As mentioned above, she considered, for example, that Lesley's ability to play melody for the children on her recorder was a quite different experience for the children than using a tape of music would have been: 'If a teacher's there with a recorder and holding that recorder and playing that pure sound from a recorder in a room where there's a focused attention, that is a very, very different experience to listening to taped popular kids' music.' Our observation of the children's complete, absorbed attention when Lesley played her recorder for them supports this view. Similarly, our observations of other instances of the children's responses to direct, personal music-making by adults in their environment indicates that this is the case – such as the observation of the children's intent attention when their teachers sang for them at an assembly, an event that was outside their usual experience.

Diverse approaches

The director also considered that a benefit deriving from the employment of musician/teachers was that they brought their own particular contribution, by virtue of their lives as adult musicians: 'And there's another component here … it's the teacher's belief and value system and her personal commitment to, and her love of, that sound too and to be able to communicate that passion to the children.' Each of the musicians in this story was able to offer this to the centre in her own way, and with surprising diversity. We could speculate that this diversity in approach and viewpoint would be unlikely to be available had the centre employed teachers trained in early childhood education expectations, a process that, to an extent, filters the individual experiences of a musician through the expectations of educational theory and practice, by providing another framework to influence the way an adult works with children. Consequently, each musician provided a unique, characteristic approach that reflected and modelled their life as an adult musician for the children. This was in accordance with the possibilities suggested by the Reggio Emilia approach. The nature of the diversity made available to the centre through the work of these musicians is discussed more fully below.

Mutual influences

The director reflected on the ways in which the musicians both influenced and were influenced by the centre's interests and activities. She framed it as a tension between the collective and individualism:

> It's about collective versus individualism and how the tension that exists there between the intent of a single teacher and what's happening in the collective. And I think that each of those [musician]/teachers were … influenced by the larger collective [about] what was happening in the centre as a whole.

She felt that Lesley, for example, who had not worked with such young children before, 'absorbed the culture, you know, she absorbed the established aesthetics, she took it on, she embraced it, she made it her own'. Similarly, she considered that Leah and Kylie were changed by their experience of working at the centre. Kylie, for example, while working with the children in one of the rooms making musical instruments, altered her teaching plans to accommodate what was happening with the children, an approach that was different from her inclination to follow her carefully designed plans in her own earlier sessions in the music space in the gallery.

The influence of the musicians on the centre is perhaps more clearly discerned in our story. The special music space developed by Lesley, the work Leah did with teachers to encourage singing and ownership of shared song repertoire across the centre and Kylie's collaboration with Suzana are all clear examples. That the director perceived that the influence went both ways suggests a more subtle and complex benefit. As the musicians absorbed the culture of the centre, their practice with the children evolved, and their influence on the programme also changed accordingly. This subtle interchange could be considered a way of breaking down some of the existing barriers between a seemingly separate music programme and the rest of the centre. This was a benefit for the centre.

Connection to the children's rooms and who should teach music: an ongoing discourse

The director considered that the responsibility of the musician teacher should be two-fold. The children attended specialist music sessions with the musician teacher once a week, which she considered was not enough.

> So the specialist teacher in the early learning centre is a person who actually has a dual responsibility, a responsibility to the children but also responsibility to those teachers who attend that class as well, to help those teachers to learn the songs and to develop their own musicality as the programme is unfolding.

Our story indicates that the extent to which the kind of connection was occurring varied. She suggested that there was a level of resistance on the part of the teachers to taking responsibility for integrating what they were observing during music sessions into their programmes in their own rooms. The musicians were aware of the difficulties in this process, and the director thought that this was a source of some frustration for them.

This, of course, varied from teacher to teacher and was probably more marked at the start of the music research. Clearly, Suzana, as a master teacher, understood the powerful potential of having a collaborative process between the teacher and the musician, allowing the boundaries between the children's experiences in the weekly music session and their daily programme in their own room to become less well defined. It is reasonable to assume that the particular story that evolved around Suzana's involvement with Kylie's work with *The Magic Flute* was a happy coincidence of events: Suzana's interest in and passion for arts education and its role in the education of young children and her skills as a teacher meant that Kylie's rather unusual work with the children found an enthusiastic and skilful advocate who was able to enrich the children's experience through her own teaching. As the director said, however, this particular relationship was not one that was typical between the teachers and the musicians, although we noted other teachers were more involved in the music programme as the research went on; through the staff singing group and through choosing to sing shared repertoire with the children, for example. The fact remains, however, that the level of involvement between Suzana and Kylie was remarkable.

Leah's interest in overcoming the barriers between the music programme and the rooms led her to work with the staff through the staff singing group, wanting to increase their confidence in themselves as singers, and wanting to help provide familiar song repertoire across the centre. Later, she worked in the rooms, bringing music into that environment, exploring the possibilities when music provision is removed from its separate and 'special place'. Later, Ray, one of the home-room teachers, asked if she could take on responsibility for the music at the centre. Although Ray's work is outside the scope of this story, her work, like Leah's, demonstrates an ongoing exploration of this concern at the centre.

The centre was exploring solutions for a long-running problem in music education, in both primary school education and, more recently, in early childhood education. The discourse about the role of specialist teachers is a long-running one; in fact, at the start of the research we were particularly interested in exploring the opposing claims made on each side of the debate. The debate is sometimes considered around the question of who should teach music. Some educators, including music educators, believe that music, as a particularly specialised skill, should be the domain of the trained music educator. Others consider that, if music is to be an integral part of a child's education, the general teacher should be assisted to take on this responsibility. Some think that this second position is best reached by the specialist teachers assisting the generalists by example and careful support. It is likely that the educators in the centre held a range of views on this issue; some may have altered their view as a result of the music project over the ten years. The director, acknowledging that the issue is a difficult one, terms this the 'elephant in the room', and feels that the nature of these tensions has not really been unpacked in this research. Nevertheless, the issue has been canvassed throughout this story.

Aim 4: arts as human experience

This topic of the significance of the arts as an important part of human experience is associated with the fourth aim of the book, which explores the notion of arts and human experience, as well as the Reggio Emilia idea of the arts having citizenship rights. These two facets of the topic are picked up here. In this book, we have explored the unfolding of a specialist music curriculum within an arts-based early childhood programme. The individual approaches of three musicians indicated how an arts-based early childhood curriculum can have different forms – all within the parameters of the centre's aims and objectives. The children's active participation and how they became protagonists in their learning have been discussed and the roles of other actors – one generalist teacher, the director, the researchers and an emerging new model of teacher/musician – have been introduced here. Major influences on the establishment of the programme in the ELC were those of the Reggio Emilia approach to early childhood education and the emergent curriculum. An essential tenet of the Reggio Emilia approach is the concept of the image of the child. The director of the ELC shared this view.

> I think the most influential principle of reaffirming children's competence is around having an image of the child as being competent in the first instance and having the capacity to absorb quite abstract ideas and to integrate those ideas through their perceptual apparatus and reach a point where they understand them.

The idea of music also being accorded citizenship rights was promoted. As mentioned above, the director felt that music needed its own uncluttered space to allow the children to experience it in its pure form.

Pursuing this theme, we asked the director why musicians had not been involved initially in the specialist arts agenda. There had not been any definite plan to not include musicians, she said, but the initiative was just developing and they utilised the talent available. The director has a background in dance, her assistant was a visual artist and another colleague from the university, also a visual artist, was researching in the area of children's expressive use of the visual arts. The parents were so enthusiastic about the arts programme that the director quickly realised she would have to formalise the arts practices by funding them separately from the everyday running of the centre because 'we saw the benefits of those specialist programmes, parents loved them and then all the arts got on board. But it was very much – it was quite organic ... people just appeared.'

One of the people who appeared was Lesley, working as an assistant in the centre, while Leah, studying for a teaching qualification at the university, heard about the arts focus at the ELC and visited with her resumé, to express an interest in teaching music. Kylie was a parent at the centre; the final music specialist, Ray, was a home-room educator who stepped forward to volunteer when Kylie left. She had musical skills, although no formal present association with music outside the ELC. The music, the director said, is now part of the culture, so, although it grew serendipitously, it now needs to be supported.

> We were lucky. But if they hadn't been there (Lesley, Leah, Kylie) and if Ray goes, she would have to be replaced. Like, now it's entrenched. So although it just grew organically and as we grew it sort of grew too and now, as the contents have grown from what it was initially to what it is now, so we're growing alongside each other in our understandings of what the curriculum would even include.

For the children, supplying them with musical experiences was seen as a child's right; the centre had a 'duty of care' to perform this duty.

> You see the impact of society and rapidly changing family lives on children's opportunities to experience music. Therefore, once again, it brings us back to the duty of care requirement that we have as educators to make certain that children have first-hand experience. It is first-hand experiences, going back to John Dewey, that those classes provide. The greater good is about the community for learners, Barbara Rogoff's notion of the practice of participation, all of us there together, experiencing our learning together and the power that is experienced when multiple people feel it at the same time. So when you're in a music class and you're focusing on the recorder, you're experiencing all that.

It was interesting that the director chose to come back to the recorder as a metaphor for the music. The researchers who observed Lesley's recorder playing with the children had also experienced these moments as powerful and quite magical. The single clear notes, the children's absolute stillness is still a strong memory.

The director was equally committed to the idea of arts having citizenship rights. She also referred to her own research.

> So, I guess, philosophically there was once again a commitment which was articulated in the vision of the early learning centre to ensure that children had the opportunity to learn in a multi-modal way and music was one of those modes or a language, another language, if you wanted to use the 100 languages metaphor. To achieve that, we needed a committed and passionate teacher of music who was going to enjoy exploring music learning with children. The notion of the argument that the arts are an important part of human experience and should be accorded citizenship rights in early childhood programmes is definitely something that came through in my research.

She went on to frame her beliefs about children's rights and rights to music in the language of the United Nations *Convention on the Rights of the Child* (*CRC*), specifically 'General Comment 7' (*CRC*, 2006). She felt that the duty of care to provide children with the language of music was also embraced in the Australian Early Childhood Code of Ethics, as promulgated by the Early Childhood Australia (ECA) group.

These comments indicate a number of important factors relating to the music programme in the ELC. The idea of rights for both children and music was articulated and couched in terms of both Reggio Emilia philosophy and the *CRC*. Another point to develop in the concluding discussion is the comment about the centre and the music growing together, that it is now part of the culture and cannot be stopped.

Concluding discussion

In this chapter, we heard the director's voice directly as we revisited the journey we have been on over the last ten years. The director was the designer and facilitator of many of the events that evolved and was always an active player in the projects and staff development. We have revisited our four aims and now look back on what has emerged. From the discussion above it can be seen that much of what occurred was planned, some was serendipitous and some was 'organic', in that events grew from what existed already. The aims of the research have been realised to the extent that we have been convinced of young children's competence in exploring and playing with musical concepts through our observations. The impact of skilled, thoughtful, quality materials and planned experiences has been affirmed. The discussion of the role of the specialist is an ongoing one, and growing diversity with the advent of the digital world is a space to watch.

What are the lessons that emerge from these observations? The role of the arts in early childhood education should be revisited in relation to government policy and resourcing of programmes. Conversations about images of children and the function of artists, in this case musicians, in early childhood education should be actively pursued. This is probably a lesson that emerges from influences like the emergent curriculum and approaches like that of Reggio Emilia. Children's rights, the rights of the arts, are positions that should be advocated for. The use of space, projects and the documentation reported on here are all examples of well-organised, thoughtful practice. In support of music, the director said:

> We are growing a deeper understanding of music pedagogy, I think because we've got a number of teachers that have been here for quite a while now. We have done a number of things over the years. Therefore, our capacity to conceptualise music learning on a more advanced level is growing. ... You know, it's quite an exciting journey ahead.

REFERENCES

Acker, A. (2014). *Music and Movement for Young Children*. TCHE2548: RMIT Edit system.

Acker, A. (2010). Early childhood, music and diversity: Exploring the potential of music for three and four year olds. In Peter Dunbar-Hall (ed.), *The Cultural Aesthetics of Teaching*. Sydney: Sydney Conservatorium of Music. pp. 6–13 (10th Cultural Diversity in Music Education Conference: The Cultural Aesthetics of Teaching).

Acker, A. (2008). Notes on Jonathan: a child's experience of a music program in a childcare setting. *Australian Journal of Music Education*. 2. pp. 14–21.

Acker, A. and Nyland, B. Young children's musical explorations: the potential of using learning stories for recording, planning and assessing musical experiences in a preschool setting. *International Journal of Music Education*. 30(4). pp. 321–8.

Anderson, L. (2002). Kindergarten teacher's perceptions on the role of music in early childhood education. Unpublished Masters thesis, University of South Australia, Adelaide.

Australian Broadcasting Commission (ABC). *Music for Movement*, radio show, presented by H. Gell 1938–58.

Australian Broadcasting Commission/Corporation (ABC). *Playschool*, children's television show 1966–present.

Barnes, M. (2004). The use of positioning theory in studying student participation in collaborative learning activities. Paper presented at the Australian Association of Research in Education Conference. Melbourne, December. http://www.aare.edu.au/data/publications/2004/bar04684.pdf

Barrett, M. (2006). Inventing songs, inventing worlds: the 'genesis' of creative thought and activity in young children's lives. *International Journal of Early Years Education*. 14(3). pp. 201–20.

Barrett, M. (2005). Musical communication and children's communities of musical practice. In D. Miell, R. MacDonald and D. Hargreaves (eds), *Musical Communication*. Oxford: Oxford University Press. pp. 261–80.

Barrett, M. (1993). Music in the early childhood classroom: an expressive medium. *Australian Journal of Early Childhood*. 18(4). pp. 23–9.

Bayless, K. and Ramsey, M. (1991). *Music: A Way of Life for the Young Child*. New Jersey: Pearson.

Beliavsky, N. (2006). Revisiting Vygotsky and Gardner: realizing human potential. *Journal of Aesthetic Education*. 40(2). Summer. pp. 1–11.

Bettelheim, B. (1989). *The Uses of Enchantment: The Meaning and Importance of Fairy Tales*. New York: Vantage.

Bond, V. (2013). Follow and facilitate: what music educators can learn from the Reggio Emilia approach. *General Music Today*. March. DOI:1177/1048371313480798.

Bond, K. and Deans, J. (1997). Eagles, reptiles and beyond: a co-creative journey in dance. *Journal of the Association for Childhood Education International*. International Focus Issue. pp. 366–71.

Bridges, D. (2008). Music with very young children: then and now. *Australian Journal of Music Education*. 2. pp. 4–14.

Brown, F. and Patte, M. (2013). *Rethinking Children's Play*. Sydney: Bloomsbury.

Bruner, J. (1991). The narrative construction of reality. *Critical Inquiry*. 18. pp. 1–12.

Bruner, J. (1975). The ontogenesis of speech acts. *Journal of Child Language*. 2. pp. 1–40.

Carlton, E. (2006). Learning through music: the support of brain research. *Community Playthings*. http://www.communityplaythings.com/resources/articles/2006/learning-through-music-the-support-of-brain-research

Campbell, P., Drummond, J., Dunbar-Hall, P., Scippers, H. and Wiggins, T. (2005). *Cultural Diversity in Music Education: Directions and Challenges for the 21st Century*. Brisbane: Australian Academic Press and the Association for Cultural Diversity in Music Education (CDIME).

Carr, M. (2001). *Assessment in Early Childhood Settings: Learning Stories*. London: Paul Chapman.

Carr, M. (2000). Technological affordance, social practice and learning narratives in an early childhood setting. *International Journal of Technology and Design Education*. 10. pp. 1–79.

Ceppi, G. and Zini, M. (eds) (1998). *Children, Spaces, Relations: Metaproject for an Environment for Young Children*. Milan: Domus Academy Research Centre.

Champion de Crespigny, M. (1958). *Easy Tunes for Music and Movement*. Melbourne: Allan and Co.

Clandinin, J. (2006). Narrative inquiry: a methodology for studying lived experience. *Research Studies in Music Education*. 27. pp. 44–54.

Clarke, H. (Comp.) (2003) *The New Useful Book: Songs and Ideas from Playschool*. Melbourne: ABC.

Clarke, H. (Comp.) (1994). *The Useful Book: Songs and Ideas from Playschool*. Melbourne: ABC.

Clark, A. and Moss, P. (2005). *Spaces to Play: More Listening to Young Children Using the Mosaic Approach*. London: National Children's Bureau.

CRC (Convention on the Rights of the Child) (2006). General Comment 7. New York: UNICEF.

Daichendt, G. (2009). Artist-teacher George Wallis: redefining the concept through history. Unpublished doctoral dissertation, Teachers College Columbia University.

Deans, J. (2008). *Antarctica: The Icy Land of Secrets*. Melbourne: Early Learning Centre, University of Melbourne (DVD).

Deans, J. and Brown, R. (2008). Reflection, renewal and relationship building: an ongoing journey in early childhood arts education. *Contemporary Issues in Early Childhood*. 9(4). pp. 339–53.

Deans, J., Brown, R. and Dilkes, H. (2005). A place for sound: raising children's awareness of their sonic environment. *Australian Journal of Early Childhood*. 30. pp. 43–7.

DEEWR (Department of Education, Employment and Workplace Relations). (2009). *Belonging, Being and Becoming: Early Years Learning Framework for Australia*. https://www.coag.gov.au/sites/default/files/early_years_learning_framework.pdf

Derham, F. (1976). *Art for the Child Under Seven*. Canberra: Australian Preschool Association.

DEST (Department of Education Science and Training). (2005). *National Review of School Music Education: Augmenting the Diminished*. Canberra: Australian Government.

de Vries, P. (2013). The use of technology to facilitate music learning experiences in preschools. *Australasian Journal of Early Childhood*. 38(4). pp. 5–12.

de Vries, P. (2009). Music at home with the under fives: what is happening? *Early Child Development and Care*. 179(4). pp. 395–405.

de Vries, P. (2006). Being there: creating music-making opportunities in a childcare centre. *International Journal of Music Education*. 24(3). 255–70.

de Vries, P. (2004). The extramusical effects of music lessons on preschoolers. *Australian Journal of Early Childhood*. 29. pp. 6–10.

de Vries, P. (2001). Reevaluating common Kodaly practices. *Music Educators Journal*. (88)3. pp. 24–7.

Dewey, J. (1944). *Democracy and Education: An Introduction to the Philosophy of Education*. New York: Free Press.

Dilkes, H. (1998). 'I was making bing and bong': children's conceptions of their own musical improvisations. *Australian Journal of Early Childhood Education*. 23. pp. 13–18.

Downie, M. R. (2003). Music education in daycare and preschool. Unpublished doctoral dissertation, Melbourne University, Australia.

Dunbar-Hall, P. (1984). *Education News*. 18. pp. 36–8.

Early Learning Centre (2014). University of Melbourne. http://elc.unimelb.edu.au/

Edwards, C., Gandini, L. and Forman, G. (1998). *The 100 Languages of Children: The Reggio Emilia Approach to Early Childhood Education*. New Jersey: Ablex.

Eisner, H. (2002). *The Arts and the Creation of Mind*. New Haven, CT: Yale University Press.

Epstein, A. (2005). *The Intentional Teacher: Choosing the Best Strategies for Young Children's Learning*. Washington, DC: National Association for the Education of Young Children (NAEYC).

Ferris, J. and Nyland, B. (2009). Researching children's musical learning experiences: learning stories, affordances and activity theory. *New Zealand Research in Early Childhood Education*. 12. pp. 81–94.

Fleer, M. (ed.) (1995). *DAPcentrism: Challenging Developmentally Appropriate Practice*. Hodder: Australia.

Fleet, A., Patterson, C. and Robertson, J. (2006). *Insights: Behind Early Childhood Pedagogical Documentation*. Baulkham Hills, NSW: Pademelon Press.

Flohr, J. (2004). *The Musical Lives of Young Children*. Upper Saddle River, NJ: Prentice Hall.

Forman, G. (1994). Different media, different language. In L. Katz and B. Cesarone, *Reflections on the Reggio Emilia Approach*. Pennsylvania: ERIC/EECE Clearinghouse. pp. 41–55.

Gardner, H. (1990). *Art Education and Human Development*. Los Angeles: Getty.

Gardner, H. (1983). *Frames of Mind: The Theory of Multiple Intelligences*. New York: Basic.

Gardner, H. (1981). Do babies sing a universal song? *Psychology Today*. 15. December. pp. 70–6.

Gatti, A. (1997). *The Magic Flute*. San Francisco: Chronicle.

Gell, H. (1949). *Music, Movement and the Young Child*. Sydney: Australasian.

Gillespie, C. and Glider, K. (2010). Preschool teachers' use of music to scaffold children's learning and behavior. *Early Child Development and Care*. 180(6). pp. 799–80.

Greaves, M. (1989). *The Magic Flute*. London: Methuen Children's.

Hands, B. P. and Martin, M. (2003). Implementing a fundamental movement skill program in an early childhood setting: the children's perspectives. *Australian Journal of Early Childhood*. 28(4). pp. 47–52.

Hanna, W. (2013). A Reggio-inspired music atelier: opening the door between visual arts and music. *Early Childhood Education Journal*. DOI 10.1007/s10643-013-0610-9.

Harris, V. (2008). Selecting books that children will want to read. *The Reading Teacher*. 61(5). pp. 426–30.

Hoermann, D. and Bridges, D. (1989). *Catch a Song*. Chicago: Incentive.

Hopkins, L. D. (ed.) (1983). *The Sky is Full of Song*. New York: HarperCollins.

Hughes, P. (2005). Baby it's you: international capital discovers the under threes. *Contemporary Issues in Early Childhood*. 6(1). pp. 30–40.

Jarmozek, M. (2010). Corridor spaces. *Critical Inquiry*. pp. 728–70.

Jones, E. (2012). *Young Children*. March. p. 67. www.naeyc.org/yc/columns.

Jones, E. and Nimmo, J. (1994). *Emergent Curriculum.* Washington, DC: National Association for the Education of Young Children (NAEYC).

Kalmar, M. (1989). The effects of music education on the acquisition of some attribute concepts in preschool children. *Canadian Music Educator, Research Edition.* special supplement to 3(2).

Katz, L. and Chard, S. (2000). *Engaging Children's Minds: The Project Approach.* (2nd edn.) New Jersey: Ablex.

Katz, L. G. and Chard, S. C. (1989). *Engaging Children's Minds: The Project Approach.* Norwood, NJ: Ablex.

Kawulich, B. B. (2005). Participant observation as a data collection method [81 paragraphs]. *Forum: Qualitative Sozialforschung/Forum: Qualitative Social Research* [on line journal]. 6(2). May. Art. 43.

Kleiner, L. (2000). *All Kinds of Weather.* California: Warner Brothers.

Laevers, F. (2011). Experiential education: making care and education more effective through well-being and involvement. *Encyclopedia on Early Childhood Development.* Belgium: CEECD/SKC-ECD.

Lightfoot, C., Cole, M. and Cole, S. (2005). *The Development of Children.* New York: Worth.

Lock, A. (1980). *The Guided Reinvention of Language.* New York: Academic Press.

Lowenfeld, V. (1947). *Creative and Mental Growth: A Text Book on Art Education.* London: Macmillan.

Lum, C. (2008). Home musical environment of children in Singapore. *Journal of Research in Music Education.* 2(1). pp. 101–17.

Marsh, K. (2010). *The Musical Playground: Global Tradition and Change in Children's Songs and Games.* Sydney: Oxford University Press.

Matterson, E. (1991). *This Little Puffin.* Melbourne: Penguin.

McPake, J., Plowman, L. and Stephen, C. (2012). Pre-school children creating and communicating with digital technologies in the home. *British Journal of Educational Technology.* 44(3). pp. 421–31.

Milikan, J. (2003). *Reflections: Reggio Emilia Principles in Australian Contexts.* Sydney: Pademelon Press.

Moog, H. (1976). *The Musical Experiences of the Preschool Child.* London: Schott Music.

Moorhead, G. and Pond, D. (1978). *Music of Young Children* [reprinted from the 1941–51 editions]. Santa Barbara, CA: Pillsbury Foundation for the Advancement of Music Education.

Morin, F. L. (2001). Cultivating music play: the need for changed teaching practice. *General Music Today.* 14(2). pp. 24–9.

Needham, M. (2007). Affordances: crossing the border from persona; perceptual schemas to socially mediated learning dispositions. Proceedings of the European Early Childhood Education Research Association (EECERA) Conference. Prague, 1–3 September.

Nieuwmeijer, C. (2013). 1+1=3. The positive effects of the synergy between musician and classroom teacher on young children's free music play. Unpublished Masters thesis. London: Roehampton University.

Niland, A. (2012). Exploring the lives of songs in the context of young children's musical cultures. *Min-Ad: Israel Studies in Musicology Online.* http://www.biu.ac.il/hu/mu/min-ad/12/4%20Niland.pdf

Nyland, B. and Ferris, J. (2009). Researching children's musical learning experiences: learning stories, affordances and activity theory. *New Zealand Research in Early Childhood Education.* 12. pp. 81–94.

Nyland, B. and Ferris, J. (2007). Early childhood music: an Australian experience. In K. Smithrim and R. Upitis (eds), *Listen to their Voices: Research and Practice in Early Childhood Music Education.* Vol. 3 Canadian Music Educator's Association Biennial series 'Research to Practice'. pp. 182–95.

Nyland, B., Ferris, J. and Deans, J. (2005). Music as experience: from Dewey to Rogoff. *International Journal of Early Childhood.* 11(1). pp. 125–39.

Nyland, B., Acker, A., Ferris, J. and Deans, J. (2013). How do you make a bear look like a butterfly? Exploring the Metropolitan Opera's production of Mozart's *Magic Flute* with a group of preschool children. *Australasian Journal of Early Childhood.* 38(1). pp. 29–35.

Nyland, B., Acker, A. Ferris, J. and Deans, J. (2011). Preschool children's encounters with *The Magic Flute*: Ruby's story. *International Journal of Early Years Education.* 19(3–4). pp. 207–17.

NZMOE (New Zealand Ministry of Education). (1996). *Te Whariki: Early Childhood Curriculum.* Wellington: Learning Media.

OECD (Organisation for Economic and Co-operative Development). (2006). *Starting Strong II.* http://www.oecd.org/newsroom/37425999.pdf

Page Smith, A. (2011). *The Incorporation of Principles of the Reggio Emilia Approach in a North American Preschool Music Curriculum: An Action Research.* New Jersey: Westminster Choir College of Rider University.

Piaget, J. (1962). *Play, Dreams and Imitation in Childhood.* New York: Norton.

Podmore, V. (2006). *Observation: Origins and Approaches to Early Childhood Research and Practice.* Wellington: NZCER Press.

Pope, J. (2008). Dalcroze eurhythmics in Australia: the first generation from 1918. Unpublished thesis, Monash University.

Pound, L. and Harrison, C. (2003). *Supporting Musical Development in the Early Years.* Buckingham: Open University Press.

Read, H. (1967). *Education Through Art.* London: Faber and Faber.

Rinaldi, C. (2006). *In Dialogue with Reggio Emilia: Listening, Researching and Learning.* New York: Routledge.

Robertson, J. (2006). Focusing the lens: gazing at 'gaze'. In A. Fleet, C. Patterson and J. Robertson (eds), *Insights, Behind Early Childhood Pedagogical Documentation.* Sydney: Pademelon Press. pp. 147–63.

Rogoff, B. (2003). *The Role of Culture in Development.* Cambridge, MA: Cambridge University Press.

Savva, A. and Trimis, E. (2005). Responses of young children to contemporary art exhibits: the role of artistic experiences. *International Journal of Education and the Arts.* 6(13). 22 pp.

Schiller, W. (2005). Children's perception of live arts performances: a longitudinal study. *Early Child Development and Care.* 175(6). pp. 543–52.

Shank, R. and Berman, T. (2002). The persuasive role of stories in knowledge and action. In M. Green, J. Strange and T. Brock (eds), *Narrative Impact: Social and Cognitive Foundations.* New Jersey: Lawrence Erlbaum Associates. pp. 287–314.

Simoncini, K., Lasen, M. and Rocco, S. (2014). Professional dialogue, reflective practice and teacher research: engaging early childhood pre-service teachers in collegial dialogue about curriculum innovation. *Australian Journal of Teacher Education.* 39(1). http://dx.doi.org/10.14221/ajte.2014v39n1.3

Suthers, L. (2004). Music experiences for toddlers in day care centres. *Australian Journal of Early Childhood.* 29(4). pp. 45–9.

Super, C. and Harkness, S. (1986). The developmental niche: a conceptualization of the interface of child and culture. *International Journal of Behavioural Development.* 9. pp. 545–69.

Tafuri, J. (2008). *Infant Musicality: New Research for Educators and Parents.* Surrey: Ashgate.

Taymor, J. (producer). (2010). *The Magic Flute.* (DVD). New York: Metropolitan Opera.

Teis, K. (2008). *The Magic Flute: An Opera by Mozart.* New York: Star Bright.

Tishman, S. (2008). The object of their attention. *Educational Leadership.* 25(5). pp. 44–6.

Trevarthen, C. (1998). The child's need to learn a culture. In M. Woodhead, D. Faulkner and K. Littleton (eds), *Cultural Worlds of Early Childhood.* London: Routledge. pp. 87–101.

van Manen, M. (1991). *The Tact of Teaching: The Meaning of Pedagogical Thoughtfulness.* Albany: SUNY Press; London and Ontario: Althouse Press.

VOSA (Victorian Orff Schulwerk Association) (2014) www.vosa.org

Vygotsky, L. (1978). *Mind in Society: The Development of Higher Psychological Processes.* Cambridge, MA: Harvard University Press.

Vygotsky, L. (1962). *Thought and Language.* Cambridge, MA: MIT Press.

Wenger, E. (1998). *Communities of Practice: Learning as a Social System.* www.infed.org/biblio/communities_of_practice.htm

Wien, C., Guyevsky, V. and Berdoussis, N. (2011). Learning to document in Reggio-inspired education. *Early Childhood Research and Practice.* 13(2). n.p.

Yelland, N. (2011). Reconceptualising play and learning in the lives of young children. *Australasian Journal of Early Childhood.* 36(2). pp. 4–12.

Young, S. (2009). Towards constructions of musical childhoods: diversity and digital technologies. *Early Child Development and Care.* 179(6). pp. 695–705.

Young, S. (2008a). Lullaby light shows: everyday music experience among the under twos. *International Journal of Music Education.* 26(1). pp. 33–46.

Young, S. (2008b). Collaboration between 3- and 4-year-olds in self-initiated play on instruments. *International Journal of Educational Research.* 47. pp. 3–10.

Young, S. (2004). Young children's spontaneous vocalizing: insights into play and pathways. *International Journal of Early Childhood.* 36(2). pp. 59–75.

INDEX